# NATHALIE DUPREE'S
## FAVORITE STORIES & RECIPES

# NATHALIE DUPREE'S
## FAVORITE STORIES & RECIPES

Nathalie Dupree with Cynthia Graubart

**GIBBS SMITH**
TO ENRICH AND INSPIRE HUMANKIND

First Edition
23  22  21  20  19          5  4  3  2  1

Stories © 2019 Nathalie Dupree
Recipes © 2019 Nathalie Dupree and Cynthia Graubart
Photographs © 2019 Hélène Dujardin Photography

Published by
Gibbs Smith
P.O. Box 667
Layton, Utah 84041
1.800.835.4993 orders
www.gibbs-smith.com

The stories on pages 10, 16, 36, 44, 48, 58, 66, 74, 82, 92, 96, 102, 106, 112, 144, 178 were originally published in *Nathalie Dupree's Matters of Taste,* © 1990 by Nathalie Dupree, published by Alfred A. Knopf, Inc. Some have been modified for this book.

Designed by Sheryl Dickert
Printed and bound in China
Gibbs Smith books are printed on either recycled, 100% post-consumer waste, FSC-certified papers or on paper produced from sustainable PEFC-certified forest/controlled wood source. Learn more at www.pefc.org.

Library of Congress Control Number:  2019936914
ISBN 13: 978-1-4236-5250-2

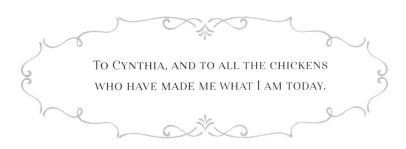

To Cynthia, and to all the chickens who have made me what I am today.

# CONTENTS

# INTRODUCTION

These are the recipes I long for, dream about, and cook regularly. Most are from ingredients I keep on hand, but some require thinking ahead and planning. Some serve a crowd and may seem pricey until the price is divided among the number of people served.

I purchase beef tenderloin when it is on sale, for instance, as I know a time will come when I will need it: an engagement party, like the one for Cynthia and Cliff so many years ago; a last-minute occasion when someone comes to this tourist-luring city of Charleston and gives us a call. Having quality ingredients on hand enables me to cook as well from the freezer—from local frozen-by-me shrimp and grits to beef tenderloin, or even sausage with the ever-present apples my husband insists on having at hand. Sides can appear frequently in season, both for just the two of us or for a crowd, as they are usually so uncomplicated they can be multiplied or divided. In a conscientious Southern household, leftovers are never for tossing but for keeping refrigerated or frozen for inclusion in desperation moments.

With an incorrigible sweet tooth, I dream of the desserts in this collection, each appearing in my mind's eye and my taste memories. My cravings vacillate from slide-down-the-throat desserts to crispy, crunchy meringues or tender cake. Growing up, we ate a lot of Jell-O and other packaged puddings, with anything else being a treat causing proportional excitement.

I've never considered myself a baker, although I have frequently baked. I am fond of certain exercises, like making pie and puff pastry, because I like the process as much as the flavor. There is something about rolling out dough that makes me happy. In fact, if I don't like the process, I don't make the dessert. So, too, I don't love doing froufrou, so you won't find much of that here. Rather, these desserts are straightforward sweets that make gluttons like me—and perhaps some of you—happy.

While the recipes are like friends, comforting and delighting me, I also refer to the richest part of my life—family and friends, who bring the most joy. The stories of food and relationships parallel the recipes. Some are stories I've told while teaching cooking classes. Others I wrote for either my column "Matters of Taste" in the *Atlanta Journal Constitution* or the *Los Angeles Times Syndicate*. A fair number were assembled into my book *Nathalie*

*Dupree's Matter of Taste,* which had a parallel TV show for the recipes but not for the stories, so they deserve a repeat view. Some appeared in periodicals such as *Brown's Guide to Georgia, Atlanta Magazine*, and the *Charleston Post and Courier.* Others are written just for this book.

I hope the stories help you to see how rich my life has been in travel, friendship, and love and leave you appreciating the good in your life. I assure you the little girl who ran away from home has found herself in a happy place, cooking good food for herself and her dear husband, Jack Bass, who will eat anything she cooks. He has come from a palate of about 3 out of 10 to a robust 8 in the twenty-five years we have been married. Both the longevity and laughter of the marriage and the growth of his palate are miracles for us both. Between us, we have written nine books in those years, this one being the ninth of our combined total of twenty-three.

Cynthia Stevens Graubart has been a dear friend since I found her when I was looking for a producer for my first television series, *New Southern Cooking.* She is in many ways the complete opposite of me, with the detailed mind of a producer and the ability to see the parts of the whole as well as the whole itself. It was a natural thing to introduce her to Cliff Graubart, who was the most eligible bachelor I knew. It was high time for him to get married and he couldn't have done better than Cynthia. I always say I'm responsible for their children, as they wouldn't have had them without me fixing Cynthia and Cliff up. There is some dispute about that. Cynthia has gone on to write and do television herself, and most likely will exceed me in the number of books she writes. She has all my secrets and those of numerous other writers, and keeps them well.

Enjoy these recipes and look for more stories and recipes to come. At eighty years old, I have more to tell, and more friends to include another time.

# THE SKINNIES AND THE ROUNDIES

Just before my twentieth high school reunion, it seemed to me the world was divided into two types of people—the skinnies and the roundies. As I talked to my high school friends on the phone or in person, I tried to determine: Were they more like a Modigliani or a Rubens? Did they jog, do aerobics, eat more than one meal a day? More importantly, what size were they? My mother always said comparisons were odious, but I found myself mentally weighing myself (literally) against my peers.

The last time I visited an old high school skinny friend (remembering her mother was a darn good cook), I nearly starved to death. Her mother is beautiful at 70, and so is my friend the skinny. She runs three miles a day, four days a week, and she was pointedly polite about my protruding stomach (although I thought I could hear her thinking "tsk, tsk" as she glanced at it). She gets a high from running. I get a high from chopping. One day I was ravenous at noon. She was surprised, saying, "But I thought you ate breakfast!" I wondered, "What has breakfast got to do with lunch?"

Thinking of a quote attributed to Catherine Deneuve, "A woman reaches an age when she must sacrifice the body for the face," I wondered if I had made the wrong choice–my face. A month away from the reunion I decided I needed to re-verse my choice and lose week weight. I was afraid all the boys in my class would remember me as a skinny, having weighed 110 pounds until just a few years ago. First I tried the sensible things. A bowl of cereal with skim milk or a boiled egg for break-fast. Low-calorie cottage cheese with slices of tomato for lunch. Poached chicken with steamed broccoli and rice or a baked potato for dinner. I sprinkled everything with herbs. Occasional fruit was my only dessert or snack. I hated it. I thought about the meals I was missing. I love food. I want to eat five times a day, if possible, small meals. I love slicing and chopping and cooking for others. I love the smells of the kitchen. I like breakfast in bed. I crave fresh food. I like to feed myself. Finally I found some recipes that satisfied my cravings and helped me lose a few pounds.

A long distance beau called, and I told him of my vows. "I," I proudly announced, hoping the declaration would spur me on as a challenge, "will be ten pounds lighter when I see you again." Instead of a crow of pleasure, I received a groan. "Oh, no," he said, "I like you Romanesque!"

With that, I threw my diet out the window. By the time of the reunion, I fit into my favorite roundies dress. I felt very comfortable in it. I got there early, quivering with anticipation at seeing people I hadn't seen for years. Like Rip Van Winkle, the years fell away. My high school sweetheart walked in the door. He'd been the high school football captain, and I suppose if you saw him today, you'd think he looked like Kenny Rogers and that he might be considered a bit beefy—a roundy, even. I

Nathalie, far left, from high school yearbook.

didn't notice. In fact, I didn't notice anyone's looks in particular, can't recall concentrating on their dresses or their shapes. All the women were beautiful, all the men handsome—just as I'd remembered them to be. The joy of being together overcame our mortality. We danced and laughed, and cried. I did notice something about the skinnies that night—in the dark you can't tell they have lines.

# BREAKFAST, BRUNCH, & LUNCH

Mealtimes and what is served when are blurring together until most anything goes, including serving breakfast for dinner. These are my sort of pantry meals—meals I always keep the ingredients for and things I can always count on to please guests. I've gained beaux from fixing omelet soufflés after the movies and have had guests swoon with pleasure when I served them for a party or crowd.

Sausage and apples has been my standby meal since the 1970s; my husband, Jack, loves it. I serve some variation of it every week. That's one nice thing about these particular recipes: they accommodate additions and substitutions, making for change-up meals. If there are recipes I cannot do without in my repertoire after all my years cooking for my family and guests, these are they.

It was hard to decide where to put shrimp and grits, because it is so easily an evening meal. But it is securely in breakfasts, as that is where it started.

# GRANNY KATE'S BISCUITS

It was a hot night, and the sun was setting later and later each day. Worrying about her grandmother, the small child couldn't sleep. She was staring at the ceiling when her mother came to tuck her in. Since she normally fell to sleep when her head hit the pillow, her mother asked if anything was wrong. "No," Jamie replied. "Are you sure?" her mother asked again. "Well," the tot replied, knowing somehow she wasn't concerned about her grandmother's mortality as much as her own self-interest, "I was just wondering—who's going to make biscuits for us when Grannie Kate dies?"

At a young age, the child had hit upon something most of us only learn late in life. There are certain foods that will linger in our memories and hearts long after the people who made them are gone. And it's important to learn from them how to make their treasures so they will live on.

Grannie Kate, still in robust good health, is the best biscuit maker I know. Her biscuits are tender, light, a bit smaller than the average, just large enough to hold sautéed pork tenderloin or a sausage without crumbling until the very end, when the juices break it up. Whenever Kate Almand is around, everyone else is tempted to take a backseat and let her make the biscuits. Although I frequently tell people she was born with a biscuit bowl in her hands, she's only been making them since she was a small child herself. One of thirteen children, she was told by her dad one day, when her mom was gone, to make the biscuits. She tried, and made a mess. The next day he had her make them again, and told her how, and she's been making them ever since.

Biscuits are quite cheap to make—just flour, baking powder, salt, and shortening in most cases, with a bit of milk or buttermilk. But it's like learning to hit a golf or tennis ball: the chances are, you aren't going to be happy until you practice a bit and study the basics.

First, the right ingredients help. Kate uses a southern soft winter wheat flour, White Lily, because it is low in protein, and that contributes to the fluffy lightness of the biscuit. She also likes Crisco better than any other shortening. She prefers sweet milk (the southern term for homogenized milk) to buttermilk, but she can make a biscuit out of any flour and shortening because she has the technique down pat.

She doesn't measure her flour. This probably goes back to the days when she bought it in huge sacks and used those sacks to make her daughter dresses. The flour, in an opened flour sack then, was as susceptible to change as it is today. In a dry season, it will absorb water differently than in a rainy one. I stopped Grannie Kate in the midst of tossing in the flour to measure her proportions so that I could give you a guide to go by until you become confident enough to wing it yourself.

When possible, she uses a biscuit bowl, larger in circumference than it is deep. She places a large quantity of flour in it, makes a well in the center, then cuts in shortening and milk in a soft motion that kneads the flour briefly as the liquid is mixed in. She winds up with a very soft dough, which she turns and coats in flour, leaving it nearly wet in the middle, but dry enough to handle on the outside. She pulls off a piece of the dough, dips the wet portion in the flour, and rolls it lightly in her floured hand. She places it on a baking sheet, keeping all the biscuits close together, so they will stay tender. When finished, she sifts any leftover flour back into a container, ready for the next day's use.

Too much kneading will make a tough biscuit. Too little will not give you as nice a rise. Too much shortening makes a crumbly dough, too little robs it of tenderness.

# TWO-INGREDIENT CREAM BISCUITS

It's miraculous to make a biscuit with only two ingredients, particularly when making such an impressive biscuit—light, tender, and capable of convincing anyone that the cook was born holding a biscuit bowl. This recipe is a good fallback for anyone who hasn't made a biscuit for a while or is in a hurry to get some baked. I prefer heavy cream (36 percent fat), but if using a cream with less fat, start with less cream and use only what is needed to make a moist, slightly sticky dough. Half-and-half just doesn't work well enough to use by itself. This is really a hurry-up recipe, but the directions are detailed; I developed them with my friend and frequent coauthor Cynthia Graubart.

These biscuits can be cut small or large. They almost float—good for butter and jam but not sturdy enough for filling with things such as ham or sausage.

MAKES 6 TO 8 (2-INCH) BISCUITS, 12 TO 14 (1-INCH) BISCUITS

2 ¼ cups commercial or homemade self-rising flour (page 20), divided

1 ¼ cups heavy cream, divided

Butter, softened or melted, for pan and finishing

Preheat oven to 450 degrees. Select a baking pan by determining if a soft or crisp exterior is desired. For a soft exterior, use an 8- or 9-inch cake pan, individual pizza pan, or an ovenproof skillet where the biscuits will nestle together snugly, creating the soft exterior while baking. For a crisp exterior, select a quarter-sheet pan or other baking pan where the biscuits can be placed farther apart, allowing air to circulate and create a crisper exterior. Butter the pan.

Fork-sift or whisk 2 cups of the flour in a large bowl, preferably wider than it is deep, and set aside the remaining ¼ cup. Make a deep hollow in the center of the flour by pressing with the back of your hand. Slowly but steadily stir 1 cup of cream, reserving ¼ cup cream, into the hollow with a rubber spatula or large metal spoon, using broad circular strokes to quickly pull the flour into the cream. Mix just until the dry ingredients are moistened and the sticky dough begins to pull away from the sides of the bowl. If there is some flour remaining on the bottom and sides of the bowl, stir in just enough of the reserved cream to incorporate the remaining flour into the shaggy, wettish dough. If the dough is too wet, use more flour when shaping.

Lightly sprinkle a flexible plastic cutting mat, wooden board, or other clean surface with some of the reserved flour. Turn the lumpy, wettish dough out onto the board and sprinkle the top of the dough

> CONTINUED

lightly with flour if sticky. With floured hands, fold the dough in half and pat it into a ⅓-to-½-inch-thick round, using a little additional flour only if needed. (If using the flexible plastic sheet, fold the sheet over itself to fold the dough.) Flour again if sticky and fold the dough in half a second time.

If the dough is still clumpy, pat and fold a third time. Pat dough into a ½-inch-thick round for normal biscuits, a ¾-inch-thick round for tall biscuits, or a 1-inch-thick round for giant biscuits. Brush off any visible flour from the top. For each biscuit, dip the biscuit cutter into the reserved flour and cut out the biscuits, starting at the outside edge and cutting very close together, being careful not to twist the cutter. The scraps may be combined to make additional biscuits, although they will be tougher.

Using a metal spatula if necessary, move the biscuits to the pan or baking sheet. Bake the biscuits on the top rack of the oven until light golden brown, about 10 to 14 minutes. After 6 minutes of baking, rotate the pan in the oven so that the front of the pan is now turned to the back, and check to see if bottoms of the biscuits are browning too quickly. If so, slide another baking pan underneath to add insulation and retard the browning. Continue baking another 4 to 8 minutes, until the biscuits are light golden brown. When they are done, remove from the oven and lightly brush the tops with softened or melted butter. Turn the biscuits out upside down on a plate to cool slightly. Serve hot, right side up.

## Homemade Self-Rising Flour

To make homemade self-rising flour, add ½ teaspoon salt and 1 ½ teaspoons baking powder to 1 cup all-purpose flour.

## Hand-shaping Methods

1. Flour hands, pull a biscuit-sized piece of dough from the mass, dip the exposed (wet) part of the dough into flour, and then roll the bottom in one floured cupped palm, simultaneously turning with thumb and pinkie while smoothing the top with the other palm. Give the dough a final pat. It's like patting one's head while rubbing one's stomach, but once the motion is clear, it gets easier each time.

2. Pat out the dough into a round of the desired height and divide into four pieces. Divide each of those into three more pieces. Roll each section between two palms to make a round. It is okay for it to be rough and bumpy.

# BASIC SOUTHERN STURDY BISCUITS

This is the basic recipe most of the biscuit makers we know use, with Cynthia's and my technique for shaping. Both Rebecca Lang's grandmother Tom and my friend Kate Almand had hands that could pull biscuits out of anything and could shape them as if by magic, just by fondling the dough. We use two different fats, for the lightness of the shortening and the flavor of the butter, as well as the enhanced browning from the butter. These are sturdy enough to hold sausage, ham, or any manner of food.

MAKES 12 (2-INCH) BISCUITS

2 ¼ cups commercial or homemade self-rising flour, page 20, divided

2 tablespoons chilled or frozen shortening, lard, and/or butter cut into ¼-inch pieces

2 tablespoons chilled butter, shortening or lard cut into ½-inch pieces

¾–1 cup milk or buttermilk, divided

Butter, softened or melted, for pan and finishing

Preheat oven to 425 degrees. Select the baking pan by determining if a soft or crisp exterior is desired. For a soft exterior, use an 8- or 9-inch cake pan, an individual pizza pan, or an ovenproof skillet where the biscuits will nestle together snugly, creating the soft exterior while baking. For a crisp exterior, select a quarter sheet pan, small baking sheet, or other baking pan where the biscuits can be placed wider apart, allowing air to circulate and create a crisper exterior. Butter the pan.

Fork-sift or whisk 2 cups of flour in a large bowl, preferably wider than it is deep, and set aside the remaining ¼ cup. Scatter the ¼-inch pieces of chilled fat over the flour then work in by rubbing between thumb and fingers as if snapping (or use a pastry cutter or two forks or knives) until the mixture looks well crumbled. Scatter the ½-inch pieces of chilled fat over the flour mixture and continue snapping thumb and fingers together, the quicker the better, until no pieces remain larger than a pebble. Shake the bowl occasionally to allow the larger pieces of fat to bounce to the top of the flour, revealing the largest lumps that still need rubbing. If this method takes longer than 5 minutes, move the bowl to the refrigerator for 5 minutes to chill the fat.

Make a deep hollow in the center of the flour by pressing with the back of a hand. Slowly but steadily stir ¾ cup of the milk into the hollow, and with a rubber spatula or large metal spoon, using broad circular strokes, quickly pull the flour into the milk. Mix just until the dry ingredients are moistened and the lumpy, sticky dough begins to pull away from the sides of the bowl.

> CONTINUED

If there is some flour remaining on the bottom and sides of the bowl, stir in 1 to 4 tablespoons of the remaining ¼ cup milk, just enough to incorporate any remaining flour into a shaggy, wettish dough. If the dough is too wet, use more flour when shaping.

Lightly sprinkle a flexible plastic cutting mat, a board, or other clean surface with some of the reserved ¼ cup flour. Turn the lumpy wettish dough out onto the board and sprinkle the top of the dough lightly with flour. With floured hands, fold the dough in half and pat it into a ⅓-to-½-inch-thick round, using a little additional flour only if needed. (If using the flexible plastic sheet, fold the sheet over itself to fold the dough.) Flour again if necessary and fold the dough in half a second time. If the dough is still clumpy, pat and fold a third time. Pat dough into a ½-inch-thick round for normal biscuits, a ¾-inch-thick round for tall biscuits, or a 1-inch-thick round for giant biscuits. Brush off any visible flour from the top. For each biscuit, dip the cutter into the reserved flour and cut out the biscuits, starting at the outside edge and cut close together, being careful not to twist the cutter. The scraps may be combined to make additional biscuits, although they will be tougher. For hand shaping and other variations, see page 20.

Using a metal spatula if necessary, move the biscuits to the pan or baking sheet. Bake the biscuits on the top rack of the oven until light golden brown, about of 10 to 14 minutes. After 6 minutes of baking, rotate the pan in the oven so that the front of the pan is now turned to the back. Lift one or two biscuits to see if the bottoms are browning too quickly. If so, slide another baking pan underneath to add insulation and retard browning. Continue baking another 4 to 8 minutes, until the biscuits are light golden brown. When they are done, remove from the oven and lightly brush the tops with butter. Turn the biscuits out upside down on a plate to cool slightly. Serve hot, right side up.

# BREAKFAST SHRIMP & GRITS

Shrimp lovers do their best to cook shrimp in the shell, as it has a natural fat that protects the shrimp and gives it extra flavor. Decide whether to peel the shrimp before or after cooking; if cooking in the shell, you may want to simmer them instead of sautéing. It is also possible to cook raw peeled shrimp in the piping hot grits.

SERVES 4

1 pound raw shrimp

4 cups water, milk, or broth

1 cup uncooked grits, preferably stone-ground

6 tablespoons butter, divided

Salt

Freshly ground pepper

If you are planning to sauté the shrimp, peel them and set aside. If simmering with shells on, see Note on page 26.

Heat the water, milk, or broth over medium heat in a medium-heavy saucepan, preferably nonstick. Slowly stir the grits into simmering liquid and cook as package directs, stirring constantly. Do not let it "blurp" loudly, as it will "spit," and watch the evaporation of liquid, adding more if necessary. When fully cooked to the desired texture, remove from heat and add 2 tablespoons of the butter and 1 teaspoon salt.

Meanwhile, heat 4 tablespoons butter in a frying pan over medium heat and sauté the peeled shrimp in the butter until they turn pink. Add the rest of the butter to the pan and melt. Top the grits with the shrimp and pour the butter on top. Taste and add more salt and pepper as needed

**VARIATION:** My favorite method of cooking grits is in the microwave in a two- or three-quart measuring cup with a handle, called a "batter bowl." The ultimate ratio is at least 4 parts liquid to 1 part grits. I usually begin with about half of the liquid, leaving plenty of room in the batter bowl so the grits don't splash or boil over. Bring the requisite amount of liquid to the boil in the batter bowl in the microwave. Stir in the grits slowly, and microwave for 5 minutes. After 5 minutes, add salt and stir vigorously to make sure there are no lumps or clumps, pushing the grits against the side of the bowl if necessary to smooth them out. Continue to cook and stir at 5-to-10-minute intervals, adding liquid as needed, until grits are cooked through and soft. (Cooking time in the microwave depends on volume, so the timing changes with the amount of food.)

> CONTINUED

If it is necessary to stop cooking midway, allow grits to cool down, then cover and refrigerate. After a few hours or up to 2 days, cook in microwave until desired texture, adding liquid as necessary. Covering the bowl will speed the cooking, but always mind the steam when removing the bowl and its cover. Plastic wrap should have an open space for steam to escape, and the grits should be removed from the bowl with care, particularly if cooking 30 minutes or more. To finish the recipe, prepare the shrimp as above.

**NOTE:** To simmer unpeeled shrimp, add enough water to a pot to cover the shrimp, and bring water to the boil over high heat. Add the shrimp. Bring back to the boil and cook until pink or until the shrimp begin to curl. If unsure, remove one and peel it. Drain and run under cool water. Peel the shells, starting with removing the legs first, or using a special shrimp peeling gadget.

**TIP:** Raw peeled shrimp can be stirred vigorously into very hot cooked grits and the hot grits will cook the shrimp.

# CLASSIC OMELET

There are as many opinions about what makes a perfect omelet as there are for all egg cooking methods. In a class at a French cooking school, I was taught that omelets should be free of any specks of brown. To me, a bit of brown gives flavor. Some like them moist and slightly runny in the center; others don't. Make your own decisions. Water makes the omelet lighter. Milk toughens an omelet. Add salt at the end, as it also toughens.

SERVES 1

2 tablespoons butter

3 eggs

1–2 tablespoons water

Salt

Freshly ground black pepper

Heat the butter in a very heavy 8-inch frying pan until it sizzles and sings. Whisk the eggs with the water in a small bowl until frothy. Pour into the hot fat to cover bottom of the pan. Use a heatproof rubber spatula to give the eggs a good stir. Remove spatula. Let eggs cook and set 1 to 2 minutes. Quickly push aside the set portion with the spatula, simultaneously tipping the pan so the raw portion runs under the cooked portion. Let eggs set again, and repeat, pushing and tipping the pan. Repeat the process one or two more times. Fluffy, soft layers of egg will build up. Holding the handle of the pan in one hand, and a plate in the other, tip the pan and slide half of the omelet out of the pan onto the plate. (If filling the omelet with grated cheese or other fillings, add them now.) Turn the pan in a slow flipping motion to fold the remaining portion on top, forming a half-moon on the plate. Season to taste with salt and pepper.

For a traditional omelet, after practicing with the two-flip omelet, try sliding one-third onto the plate, cover with the second third, and slide the third side under, jiggling the plate.

Variations abound, including adding herbs and other ingredients to the eggs, and filling with grated cheese, ham, chicken, etc. The sky is the limit.

# God Bless the Egg Man

I can only relate the children of furloughed and/or unpaid workers to my own experience. One time when I was twelve years old, the egg man, who delivered a dozen or two eggs each week, the milkman, who left milk products in a lightly insulated silver-colored box, and the bread man supported us for a month. We were four in our family, and we split half of my father's Army Colonel salary. My mother was a divorced woman. She had learned to type after my father left, went to short-hand school at night, and got a job at the lowest grade in the government. She never made much money or got a higher grade, but she did get in-grade raises, which she felt put her in good stead over the years. She also had a second job on Thursday nights and Saturdays selling at Jellef's, a small department store in Shirlington, Virginia.

I remember having heard about government hiring freezes from time to time when the Congress instituted a no-hiring ban on parts or maybe all of the government. Mother would say things to us like, "There's a freeze on at Navy." That would mean there was no sense trying for a job in that department, as they could not hire. And if you were hired but hadn't started working, you couldn't start. Mother's government office had closed and she was about to start in another department on Monday. And then it happened: There was a hiring freeze mid her job transition.

Mother had been promised that job, given a date to start, and assumed she would have work. Instead, she only had her part-time department store job and my father's child support payments, then called the allotment. My father was a finance officer, and every once in a while he would manipulate the payments so they would be delayed, because he resented supporting us. He never quite understood that four of us lived on what one of him lived on. And his wife worked.

When we didn't receive the allotment on time, mother's checks would bounce, the bank would charge her more, and the amount we didn't have would compound itself so that it ate into what we should have had to live on. And so we depended on the milkman, the bread man, and the egg man. There were no credit cards in that day, but these men would issue monthly credit. They weren't happy issuing us credit, as my mother was a divorced woman, but they did.

The second mother found out she didn't have that job, she immediately left a note in the milk box and on the door and ordered as many eggs and milk as she could. We filled the refrigerator with them. What we ate all those weeks was eggs. We had a little butter, and when that was gone it was gone. But those eggs, they were there every day to be boiled. Without butter, the eggs would stick if cooked any other way.

We had some tuna fish, some Dinty Moore stew and other canned goods for a little while, but it ran out too. After a period of time, the bread man and the milkman wouldn't leave us any more. But the egg man kept leaving eggs. He felt sorry for us. We got an eviction notice on the front door. This had happened before, but this time it felt ominous. And it was always embarrassing when our friends saw it.

Mother walked through the woods to the store to work as many days as she could. But she had to take the bus home in the dark. One night she came home in tears. It was cold, and she had walked through the woods home in the dark. She had cried all the way home. She had been fired from the store. There was finally nothing to eat, no money for us to take the bus to school or her to get home that night, and she had already borrowed from everyone she could at church. In desperation, she had taken five dollars from the register. They caught her in the act, she was so inept at stealing, as she didn't know what to do or how to do it. She had every intention of repaying it, but who doesn't? And so she took her purse and walked home in the dark, weeping. I felt so sorry for her, trying to do the right thing for us, the wrong thing for God, maybe, and the shame of being caught.

# OMELET SOUFFLÉ

Omelet soufflés are a base of egg yolks lightened with beaten egg whites, cooked in the oven in an omelet pan or a small nonstick frying pan. They can be savory or sweet, served filled or unfilled depending on the occasion.

SERVES 2

6 large eggs, separated

¼–½ teaspoon salt

Freshly ground black pepper

½ teaspoon cream of tartar (optional)

2 tablespoons butter

Fillings, if desired, see below

Preheat oven to 375 degrees.

Whisk the egg yolks in a large bowl with salt and pepper to taste, until thick.

Whisk the egg whites and cream of tartar, if using, to soft peaks in a large bowl. Gently fold in a large spoonful of the yolk mixture to soften the egg whites. Fold this mixture into the rest of the yolks until just incorporated. Be careful not to overmix, as doing so will deflate the whites.

Melt the butter in a 9- or 10-inch nonstick, ovenproof skillet. If unsure, wrap the handle of the skillet with aluminum foil. Pour in the egg mixture and immediately move to the oven. Bake 10 to 12 minutes, or until the soufflé is fluffy and golden brown. While the soufflé is cooking, prepare any filling.

Immediately after removing the omelet soufflé from the oven, loosen the edges with a spatula. Slide omelet onto a heated plate; add the filling, fold over the top, and press lightly with the bottom of the pan. Top with a sprinkle of the filling, if desired. Serve immediately, dividing in two at the table.

**FILLINGS:** For a savory filling, try ½ cup grated cheddar cheese, ½ cup soft goat cheese, sautéed mushrooms, or a crisp fresh vegetable. For a sweet omelet soufflé, add a tablespoon of sugar to the egg whites, and fill with berries or sliced peaches mixed with 1 tablespoon of warmed red currant jelly. Omit the black pepper. Sprinkle with confectioners' sugar.

# CHEESE SOUFFLÉ

The soufflé dish is an important way to bring glamour to the table. Too large a dish will make it appear it didn't rise; a small dish may be "enlarged" by adding a collar of parchment paper or foil—removed before serving—to hold the soufflé as it rises.

SERVES 4 TO 6 FOR LUNCH

4–5 tablespoons butter, divided

Breadcrumbs or panko

4 tablespoons all-purpose flour

1 ½ cups milk, preferably Flavored Milk (page 34)

1 ½ cups grated cheese

1 teaspoon Dijon mustard

Dash of freshly grated nutmeg, optional

Dash of ground hot red pepper

6 large eggs, separated

Salt

Freshly ground black pepper

2 additional egg whites

⅛ teaspoon cream of tartar

Measure the soufflé dish with water first, just to check the amount it holds.

Preheat oven to 400 degrees. Position a rimmed baking sheet in the center of the oven with no racks above so the soufflé can rise unimpeded. The hot metal will give the soufflé a boost from the bottom as well as catch any dribbles.

Butter a 4- or 5-cup soufflé dish with 1 to 1 ½ tablespoons of the butter and dust it with fine, dry breadcrumbs or panko. If the dish appears to be too small to hold all the soufflé mixture, fold a long sheet of foil or parchment paper in half lengthwise, butter and crumb, and tie with twine around the outside of the dish, extending the height of the dish. Put a serving plate next to the stove area to hold the finished soufflé dish so it is easier to move.

Melt the remaining butter in a heavy saucepan over medium heat. Add the flour and stir briefly until smooth. Add the milk all at once. Stir with a wooden spoon until the mixture comes to the boil and is smooth. Add the cheese, mustard, nutmeg, and hot red pepper and mix together. Remove from the heat and add the 6 egg yolks one at a time, mixing well after each addition. Season liberally with salt and pepper, remembering the egg whites are yet to be added.

> CONTINUED

This cheese sauce may be prepared in advance to this point and stored in the refrigerator or frozen. If letting the mixture rest, cover with plastic wrap or coat with a light sprinkle of grated cheese to avoid a film forming on top. If refrigerating or freezing, reheat sauce gently before proceeding.

Beat the 8 egg whites and cream of tartar in a clean, dry bowl of a stand mixer fitted with a rotary whisk, an electric hand mixer, or by hand with a balloon whisk, until they are shiny and form a firm peak. If using a small hand mixer, use as large a bowl as possible, circling the mixer around the bowl. Stop after the peaks just begin to form and beat the last few minutes by hand if possible. Underbeating the eggs is better than overbeating them, causing the air bubbles to burst. Stop beating before the eggs look rough and "rocky."

Use a spatula or large metal spoon to fold about 1 cup of beaten egg white into the warm sauce to soften. Pour the sauce over the remaining egg whites, folding it in until nearly completely integrated. The last few pockets of egg whites will disappear as the soufflé bakes. (This may be done up to several days in advance, with the soufflé brought up to room temperature before baking, although it will have less height.)

Pile the soufflé mixture carefully into the prepared dish. It should fill the dish within an inch of the top. Any extra mixture can be added, if a collar is used, to slightly above the rim. (Or cover and refrigerate extra mixture, then bake in the next few days in smaller ramekins.) Smooth the top. Run a knife quickly around the inside of the dish to aid the soufflé's release later. If desired, run a knife around in a circle around the middle of the top of the soufflé mixture to allow a "cap" to form while baking. This will rise separately and enhance the presentation.

Move the dish to the middle of the hot baking sheet. Immediately turn the oven down to 375 degrees. Bake 20 minutes, or until the soufflé has risen. Open the oven door, reach in and touch the top of the soufflé. If it is soft on top, close the oven door and continue to bake. Recheck in 5-minute increments. When it is done, it will be lightly firm on top, and a skewer inserted into it will have a small amount of soufflé on it when removed. Remove the soufflé dish from the oven and put the dish on the serving plate. If using a collar, snip off the string and remove the collar carefully. If it starts to stick, hold a knife outside the collar to use as a firm guide, and move it around the dish while peeling off the paper. Discard paper and string.

After quickly showing off the soufflé, immediately use two large spoons inserted back to back into the center of the dish to "open" the soufflé. It should have a small pool of sauce *baveuse* in the center. If the soufflé is moderately runny, start serving, moving around the outside edges of the soufflé dish. The center will continue to cook and should be perfect in a few minutes. If the soufflé is still very runny, it may be returned to the oven until it firms a bit, just a few minutes, before or after serving the outside edges.

> CONTINUED

If the soufflé falls, it has been overbaked, causing the air bubbles so carefully beaten into the eggs to overexpand and burst. Run a knife around the inside rim of the collar-free soufflé dish. Invert the serving plate over the soufflé dish and flip the soufflé and the dish over. Give a quick, firm shake. If properly buttered and crumbed, the bottom and sides will release. Serve on the dish. No need to tell anyone it fell. It will be slightly denser than a regular soufflé and more like a light custard. Call it a twice-baked soufflé, or say nothing and just enjoy the raves.

# FLAVORED MILK

Technically a milk stock, Flavored Milk adds an underlying flavor to any dish. I make this when I have just a little milk in a carton to finish off and some bits and pieces of vegetables. Adding a chicken bone or a meat scrap will make it even better.

MAKES 1 ½ CUPS

| | |
|---|---|
| 1 ½ cups milk | Thyme, parsley stalk, as desired |
| 1 slice onion | 1 slice fennel bulb |
| 1 slice celery | Peppercorns, as desired |
| 1 slice carrot | Chicken bone or meat scrap, if desired |

Heat milk over medium heat in a saucepan on the stove, or in a glass measuring cup in the microwave, with any of or all of the above ingredients until warm and nearly at a simmer. Remove from heat and let sit ½ hour at room temperature or longer in the refrigerator. Strain before using. The flavored milk will last, covered in the refrigerator, as long as the milk is good. Add it to any milk-based sauce such as a béchamel or cheese sauce.

**VARIATION, TWICE-BAKED SOUFFLÉS:** Butter 6 (5- or 6-ounce) ramekins and preheat oven to 375 degrees. Make soufflé as directed, and ladle evenly into the prepared ramekins. Place a clean tea towel in the bottom of a large shallow baking pan. Move the filled ramekins to the pan lined with a tea towel. Move to the oven and carefully, without splashing the ramekins, add boiling hot water to the pan until the water reaches halfway up the sides of the ramekins. Using boiling hot water speeds up the time it takes to heat the pan water and start the cooking. Lower the heat to 350 and bake 20 minutes or so, depending on the size of the ramekins. The soufflés are done when the tops are lightly firm and a skewer inserted into the soufflé still has mixture clinging to it. Remove the baking pan holding soufflés carefully from the oven; then remove soufflés from the bath and let collapse and cool. Cover with plastic wrap and refrigerate up to 3 days, or leave at room temperature up to 1 hour.

To serve, preheat oven to 350 degrees. Top soufflés with 1 cup grated Parmesan cheese. Bake 15 to 20 minutes, until soufflés have risen again and turned slightly golden brown. Remove from oven and serve immediately.

**VARIATION, TWICE-BAKED SOUFFLÉS WITH CREAM SAUCE:** Heat 1 cup heavy cream, 3 seeded and chopped tomatoes, and 1 tablespoon chopped fresh tarragon in a small saucepan over medium heat. Season to taste with salt and pepper to make a sauce. Butter a dish large enough to hold the unmolded soufflés together in a single layer. Run a knife around the insides of the ramekins and turn out the cooled, baked soufflés into the prepared dish. (If one comes out unevenly, don't worry; just push it back together.) Divide the sauce and 1 cup grated Parmesan cheese evenly over the soufflés. Bake 15 to 20 minutes, until soufflés have risen again and turned slightly golden brown. Remove from the oven and spoon each soufflé onto a warm plate. Spoon any remaining sauce on top.

# A Special Family Breakfast

They'd been divorced nearly forty years when my father phoned me, asking me to help him see his former wife, my mother, together with the rest of their children. His second wife and her second husband were now dead and each of my parents was alone.

Surprisingly, my mother agreed to the meeting, "for the sake of the children." Her rancor at having been left with three demanding children had cooled in the slow oven of time and now it rarely flared, only sizzled.

He had suggested they have breakfast—his favorite meal—at his local diner. He was now 82 and rose before dawn, finishing eating before the sun was up. On those rare occasions when he waited until seven or eight in the morning, it was a grave concession to the rest of the world's rhythm.

My mother, now 75, still worked three days a week, for the church library. In her heart of hearts, she thought the world would be a better place if everyone slept a bit later (at least until dawn), ate breakfast after sunrise, and came gently into the world each morning, only after reading and praying.

I knew that diner only too well, for that is where I had met him many times at barbaric hours of the morning, for grits and eggs and bacon. They served cheap margarine, and the waitresses parceled out the sugar and Sweet'n Low packets from their apron pockets only upon request. There was always a crowd there, always a din, with salesmen calling to each other across the red vinyl booths.

What kind of meal, what kind of place, should it be for all the family to meet, forty years later? Surely a place where they wouldn't have to shout. Because if they started to shout, only to be heard, maybe it would continue, their voices rising distinct over the cacophony, spiraling above them all with the stifled angers of bygone years.

No, it had to be a place where the atmosphere would temper those feelings if that pot was uncovered. It had to be at an hour when the crowds were sparse, when the world had already moved into its daily rhythm. The place had to serve butter, the bread had to be warm.

We children, grown, terrified of the event, had to be able to leave without bolting, if the pain became too great. But what if they all left? Who would pay the check in the swirl of emotions?

It was agreed. We would all get together at a small, elegant hotel at nine in the morning. We met in the gilded lobby and proceeded to the dining room, where, mercifully, we were greeted expeditiously and seated in the rear of the room.

He ordered the same breakfast he always had nearly every day of his life. Mother was swept up by the occasion, the splendor of the room, the length of the menu. She vacillated, unsure of what would be the best, wanting to remember the best. We children ordered the safest items. No crumbled croissants for them.

Breakfast came. The bread was hot, the butter was real. It melted easily. It was to me terrifying to find we were civilized, polite, and liked each other.

"Do you miss your husband?" he asked. "Yes," she said, "he was good to me. And we had the church." She paused, then asked shyly, "Do you miss your wife?"

"Yes," he answered, "although she wasn't herself for a long time. Your husband wasn't either, was he?" "No," she said, "he didn't know me for some time."

They looked at each other from lowered eyes. We children faded, shadowed, and didn't know the people our parents had become in just a few moments. He said to her at last, "I see you still drink too much coffee." She said, "Yes" and laughed, a small, delicate bell-like laugh her children had never heard before. It even surprised her. As she raised her hand to cover her mouth, her napkin fell to the carpet. "I only drink one cup a day," he said, and stooped to retrieve her napkin. "You still have the most beautiful legs of any woman I have known," he remarked, wiping the drops of his single cup of coffee from his smile. "I've always liked your mustache," she returned, watching as his napkin left the mouth she used to know. Everyone started talking at once, sharing memories, laughing and teasing, the pot of emotions now bubbling like a good soup.

We took pictures. He called the waiter over. He was always more comfortable with strangers than intimates. "This is my family," he said. "These are my children. This is their mother. And this is the first time we've all been together in forty years." The waiter smiled politely and took more pictures for us.

"You did a good job with the children," my father said. Turning to us children, she said, "God helped me, they are my jewels."

He called for the check and said, "Next time, let's go to my favorite diner. A bit earlier. I can't afford this expensive restaurant again." She smiled and nodded her head as he took her arm and walked her to the car, we children only moments behind, dazed with the wonder of it all. We were a family. Maybe we always had been.

# CARAMELIZED ONIONS

Once I had a cooking student from a nearby town, Monroe, Georgia. She came in declaring she hated to cook, but her husband wanted her to learn so she was there. She dramatically held up her hands, saying, "These hands were made to hold charge cards, not a knife." She did not return after that class. Later I saw her at a party and asked her what happened. She replied, "I learned all I needed to know—if I cooked onions and garlic, he thought I'd been home all day."

In fact, caramelized onions are the basis for many dishes, and cooking them is an important technique to learn, as onions have a high water content and are reluctant to brown. Cooked too low, they'll extrude water and never brown. Cooked too high, they lose too much water and become crisp or burned rather than tender.

MAKES ABOUT 3 CUPS

8 tablespoons butter or oil, cook's preference

8 medium onions, sliced

Salt and freshly ground black pepper

Heat the butter or oil over medium heat in a large skillet. Add the onions to the fat, reduce the heat, and add 1 teaspoon salt and a little freshly ground pepper. Cook slowly, stirring every few minutes, until the bottom of the pan becomes brown and the onions are soft and golden brown. If liquid from the onions gathers in the bottom of the pan, turn up the heat to evaporate the liquid, taking care not to burn the onions. Alternately, heat another pan with some oil or butter, and move half the onions to the hot pan so there is not a deep layer of onions, which has a propensity to steam rather than caramelize the onions. As the bottom of the pan begins to brown, stir the onions so the brown goodness on the bottom of the pan transfers to the onions. Continue cooking and stirring over low to moderate heat until soft and a golden amber color, about 35 to 40 minutes. There should be no excess liquid in the pan, and the onions should be deep brown, but not burned. Season to taste.

Hot water, stock, vinegar, or other liquid may be added and stirred over heat, bringing to the boil, to remove the remaining brown from the bottom of the pan, a process called "deglazing," which yields brown goodness for a sauce or soup. Sugar may be added at any time in the process, but a Vidalia onion in particular should not need any to be flavorful and rich.

# GOLDEN VIDALIA ONION TART WITH OLIVES & ROSEMARY

Our Georgia Vidalias are among the world's sweetest onions. This free-form tart needs no special equipment such as a tart pan with a removable bottom or a pie pan. Try experimenting with shapes like rectangles and squares so guests don't think it is "just" an onion pizza but something extraordinarily special, which it is. Store-bought piecrust is handy, but try to use a name brand and avoid using those in a flimsy tin.

MAKES 1 (11-INCH) TART

1 recipe Very Versatile Cream Cheese Dough (page 160), or 1 (9-inch) store-bought piecrust

½ recipe Caramelized Onions (1 ½ cups) (page 39)

1 cup grated Gruyère or cheddar cheese, or soft goat cheese

Freshly ground black pepper

1–2 sprigs fresh rosemary, leaves stripped and chopped

½ cup Greek or other black olives

Preheat oven to 375 degrees.

Roll the piecrust with a rolling pin on a lightly floured surface into an 11-inch-long rectangle or other shape of your choice. Move to a pizza pan or baking sheet, fold up the edges of the dough about ¼ inch all around, decorating if desired. Prick all over with a fork and chill at least 30 minutes. Move the pan and cold tart crust to the middle shelf of the preheated oven and bake until golden brown, about 10 to 15 minutes.

Meanwhile, prepare ½ recipe Caramelized Onions.

Layer caramelized onions onto the prebaked tart crust and top with cheese. Sprinkle with pepper and most of the rosemary. Reserve remaining rosemary to sprinkle on after baking. Lay the olives on a counter and swack them with the side of a large knife to loosen the pits. Remove pits, roughly chop olives, and sprinkle them on top of the rosemary and cheese.

When ready to bake, preheat oven to 375 degrees. Bake the filled tart on the middle shelf until cheese is melted and crust is a solid brown, about 10 to 20 minutes. Remove from oven. Sprinkle with remaining rosemary, if desired. Serve hot or cold.

# CARAMELIZED ONION SOUP

My meal of choice is onion soup when I go to France, arriving in the early morning from the East Coast with a stomach growling after a scanty airplane breakfast. It energizes me enough to remain awake until nighttime sleep claims me, helping me get on a schedule right from the start. Although much onion soup has a soggy bread that readily slips down the throat, perfect for warming the coldest soul and body during a rainy French day, I like floating crisp croûtes on top, perhaps making enough to accompany the soup as well as for a finishing addition.

SERVES 6 TO 8

½ recipe Caramelized Onions (1 ½ cups) (page 39)

1–2 large garlic cloves, chopped

1 tablespoon all-purpose flour

8 cups stock or broth, preferably brown (if using commercial, make with half water and half stock)

Salt

Freshly ground black pepper

6–8 thick slices French bread

1 cup mixed Swiss and grated Parmesan cheese

Using a large Dutch oven, prepare ½ recipe of Caramelized Onions.

Add the chopped garlic to the caramelized onions and cook 1 to 2 minutes more. Remove from heat and stir in the flour. Return to heat and stir constantly for 1 to 2 minutes, or until flour is cooked. Pour in the stock. Increase heat to medium high and continue stirring until stock comes to the boil. Reduce heat to a simmer and cook, partially covered, for 20 to 30 minutes. Season to taste with salt and pepper. Do not over-salt at this point or it may be too salty when reheated, particularly if using a commercial stock and the liquid is reduced. The soup may be refrigerated for several days or frozen at this point.

To prepare the croûtes, preheat oven to 325 degrees. Arrange bread slices side by side on a rimmed baking sheet, move to upper third of the oven, and toast until browned, about 15 minutes. Brush bread with oil or butter to add more flavor to the soup. These croûtes may be kept a day or so in a plastic bag.

When ready to serve, preheat oven to 375 degrees. Reheat soup on top of the stove if necessary. Arrange croûtes side by side on top of the soup in the pot or individual ovenproof bowls and sprinkle evenly with cheese. Bake soup in the middle of the oven until cheese has melted and formed a light brown crust, about 10 to 15 minutes.

# Food for Funerals

From time to time I have experienced empty places at the tables of my life. I find that when I eat certain foods that remind me acutely of someone I cared for, that person is with me again, and death's power is diluted. Food is such an integral part of friendship that when death occurs, there is a longing to use food as a final present, something to bond the living to those gone.

My friend Bert Greene left without saying goodbye to many of his friends. A giant of a man, he was vain only about his looks, and he hadn't wanted many of us to come to the hospital to see him, unshaven. In August, the "Thanksgiving friends" (those friends who were always invited as family at Thanksgiving even if they couldn't attend), gathered once again at Bert's Long Island home. Phillip Schultz, his longtime companion, hosted a small garden party there to celebrate Bert's life.

The brisket was still warm when I arrived late the night before. Phillip had marinated and smoked it that day for many a long, slow, lonely hour. I sliced off a bit of the tender, flavorful piece of meat, eating it out of hand, standing over the burnished wood kitchen table. My goodness, it was wonderful. Phillip snitched it away, exclaiming it needed Dinah's sauce. How could it be any better, I wondered. Besides, the brisket was for tomorrow's lunch, and Dinah was one of the cats!

Early the next morning, Phillip was up, making the sauce. Dinah was mostly fur surrounding a tiny frame that was more Jell-O than bones. She was not overly affectionate but wanted a great deal of attention, which was manifested in her indecision. You know the kind, always hanging at the door wanting out when she was in and in when she was out. Once, because of this distraction, some onions had burned. Phillip went ahead and made the sauce anyway, and the result was marvelous, thanks to Dinah's diversion. Hence the name, whenever I use nearly burned onions in a sauce.

We ate all day, people arriving at different hours, some going to the beach for a while, some sitting around and talking, some playing croquet, all the while tasting the foods brought in cars or, like Elizabeth Schneider's cake, on the bus from the city. Arthur Schwartz made a punch full of boozy fruit; Rose Beranbaum brought Bert's sponge cake from her new book, *The Cake Bible*. I lost, badly, at croquet, grilling the chicken in between swats of the mallet. And so the long day went.

When we were all assembled, the heat was cooling down in the back of the garden where a hole had been dug. Bert's ashes were mixed together with his sister Myra's, who had passed on a year earlier. Together again, they were planted under a star magnolia. Arthur read from a borrowed Jewish prayer book. Sue Huffman read from the Bible, still others spoke from their hearts. Some just sat on the grass, choked up with their grief, and cried.

After we had said good-bye in our own ways, we filled up our plates and sat in a circle outside near the kitchen and talked about Bert, how we met him, what he meant to us—long stories that made us laugh, others that exemplified how he gave to friends and fans when the temptation was to be churlish. We remembered the good he enabled us to pass on, his enthusiasm for life. When the late summer sun went down over the star magnolia, we parted. I ate the last of the brisket before I went to sleep, full of gratitude that Bert goes on, as he did before I met him, in his books, his recipes, and in the laughter of his friends.

# CHILLED MELON SOUP

This is a favorite soup of mine. I don't always comply with the amounts here, as melons are so variable. I use the amounts as guidelines for a simple and refreshing starter. It's hard to do the wrong thing. It's fine just to use melon juice from just one of the melons if a second isn't available, or to add vinegar, lemon juice, or other variations.

SERVES 4 TO 6

1 ½ cups ripe cantaloupe roughly cut in 1-inch pieces, seeds removed

5 cups ripe watermelon roughly cut in 1-inch pieces, seeds removed

1–2 tablespoons white wine vinegar (optional)

Purée the cantaloupe in a food processor or blender to make 1 cup of liquid. Repeat with the watermelon, making 3 cups of liquid. Taste and add the vinegar if desired. The purées can be poured separately and swirled together in the bowl for a pretty design, or they can be combined. Cover and chill thoroughly, refrigerating until ready to serve.

**VARIATIONS:**

- Add chopped mint, basil, or tarragon, as desired.

- Add a creamy goat cheese or lemon Stilton for a savory course.

- Mix with honey and fresh mint for a satisfying, cool dessert course.

# GAZPACHO

It's hard to believe there was a time when I hadn't eaten a cold soup, but such was the case when I first went to Majorca. There, I met a Danish countess who had been a beautiful opera singer at the time of World War II. Returning with the troops was the grandson of the king, heading the procession wearing a uniform and driving a convertible. She and the king's grandson met, married, and moved to Majorca. When she served this soup to me, she insisted that some of the chopped ingredients be saved to be added at the last minute to aid digestion. I follow her orders even today.

SERVES 8

2 large onions

3 large garlic cloves

2 red bell peppers, seeded and cored

1–2 small cucumbers

2 pounds ripe tomatoes, peeled and seeded, cut into chunks

½ cup crumbled biscuits or bread

3 cups tomato juice, fresh or canned

5 tablespoons red wine vinegar

Salt

Freshly ground black pepper

1 cup bread cubes, fried in 3 tablespoons butter or oil, cook's preference

Roughly cut three-fourths each of the onions, garlic, bell peppers, and cucumbers into pieces and purée in a food processor or sturdy blender, reserving the remaining one-fourth cut vegetables to be chopped and served as garnish.

Add the tomatoes and biscuits or bread and process again. Add tomato juice and vinegar as needed to process to a smooth texture. Remove as necessary to a bowl if the container becomes too full.

Pour puréed vegetables into a bowl with any remaining juice and vinegar. If too thick, ice water or more juice can be added. Season to taste with salt and pepper.

Chop the remaining onion, garlic, bell pepper, and cucumber. Chill both the soup and the garnish ingredients. When ready to serve, ladle soup into individual bowls and pass the chopped ingredients along with the fried bread cubes, to be sprinkled into each bowl. Gazpacho will last nearly a week in the refrigerator. If ripe, lush tomatoes are not available, use high-quality canned tomatoes or tomato juice (not V-8 juice).

# Love Bloomed

She always wondered if they would have fallen in love if she hadn't brought the cold soup. It had been an unusually hot day when she was leaving the house, and it had come to her that he would like the soup. The sun beat down on the flat roof above his office in the sleepy Georgia town. It would be cool and soothing for him, in contrast to the energy that radiated from him.

So she packed the soup in a plastic container and put it inside a nondescript paper bag. An afterthought, really. She figured he wouldn't have eaten lunch. Even if he had, what would it matter, it was only a bowl of soup.

It changed her life, that bowl of soup. She had served it the night before and it had been good. As she climbed the dusty staircase, the container opened a crack, and a few drops fell out on her red sundress. She flicked them off with her hand, smudging the file folder she was bringing him to review.

He never commented about the spots on the file or on her dress when he recalled that day. She remembered how hot she had been, her shoulders nearly glistening, the cotton dress clinging to her back. She had opened her slightly soiled sack on his desk, first covering the desk with a paper towel from the tiny bathroom near his office. From his office window she could see the town's main street—a dog walking across the road, her own car with the windows rolled down (she wished the car had been air-conditioned). She could hear music from the offices below.

She hadn't known she would remember it forever, the way he looked at her—as if she was beautiful—when she opened the sack. She smiled at him, telling him she had something for him. He held the plastic bowl as though it were crystal, cupping it with his hands and drawing it to his lips. If she had known she was going to fall in love with him that moment, she would have brought him a spoon.

"See what she brought me," he exalted to his coworker, "a bowl of cold soup!" The other man didn't know the soup was mystical. "Ah, yes," he replied, "I've had it before. I liked it." He gave a small nod and a tiny smile, wondering at the tension before him over a bowl of soup in the middle of the day. "*Like* it?" her new love protested. "Like it? It's marvelous! I've never had anything as marvelous before. This is remarkable!"

A small, hard, untrusting part of her, deep inside, was touched, and opened to him. After he ate the soup, they worked together, she on one side of his desk, he on the other. The sun filtered through to her work in a golden beam, moving around the room as they worked. He taught her so much that the small, hard part of her soul became plump and tender, like a raisin soaked in wine. Without a touch or a word of love, they had each given the other a new world. She never made the soup again without thinking of him.

# GOLDEN GAZPACHO WITH CHILIS & SHRIMP

Adapted from Craig Claiborne's *Southern Cooking*, I have made this many times, as much for the color as for its vibrant taste: it cools and excites the palette and palate simultaneously. Chilis vary in hotness, hence the a wide variation in amount. Search for English or other "burpless" cucumbers.

MAKES 4 CUPS (SERVES 4 TO 6)

½–1 ½ teaspoons finely chopped fresh hot chili peppers, preferably serrano

1 cup chicken stock or broth, divided

½ teaspoon saffron threads

2 tablespoons fresh lime juice

2 pounds (about 6) yellow tomatoes

⅓ cup chopped yellow bell peppers

¾ cup chopped cantaloupe

½ cup chopped mango

½ cup seeded, peeled, and diced cucumber

2 tablespoons finely chopped green onion, whites only

Salt

1 pound cooked, peeled shrimp

1 tablespoon chopped fresh cilantro

Purée half the hot pepper, ¾ cup of the chicken stock, saffron, and lime juice in a food processor or blender. Taste, and add the remaining hot pepper if desired, and purée until smooth.

Meanwhile, peel, seed, and dice the tomatoes to make about 2 cups. Toss the yellow peppers, cantaloupe, mango, cucumber, and green onions in a large bowl. An hour before serving, add the hot pepper-broth mixture and stir to blend. Taste and thin with the remaining stock if needed. Chill at least 1 hour.

Season to taste with salt. Cut each shrimp in 1 to 2 pieces. Spoon equal portions of soup into 4 to 6 chilled soup bowls. Top with shrimp and sprinkle with cilantro.

# SAUSAGE & APPLES

Although this is the base for quiches, overnight casseroles, dressings, and other dishes, my husband, Jack, and I never tire of this for a casual supper. I like leaving the apple peel on for color and nutrition, but of course it can be removed. Vegetables can be added to enhance this dish and clean out the fridge.

SERVES 4

1 pound sausage links or bulk sausage

2 red Gala apples, or other cooking apples

Fry the sausage in a large skillet until cooked through, with no pink remaining. Meanwhile, core and slice the apples into ½-inch wedges. Add the wedges to the sausage, or remove sausage if there is no room, and sauté until apples are brown, soft, and caramelized but not mushy. Drain sausage and apples on a plate lined with paper towels, if necessary. Serve hot.

**VARIATION:** Add sliced onions, baby potatoes, spinach, Brussels sprouts, or mushrooms to the fat. Brown the onions and potatoes alone in the fat; cook the other vegetables alone or with the apples until vegetables are tender.

## Cooking Sausage

Links—Prick the skins before adding to a cold pan, turn up the heat and cook until deep brown; turn and repeat until brown all over. If more than ½ inch in diameter, add a bit of water to the pan after initial browning to keep links from burning before the sausage is cooked through. Cover if necessary to ensure they are thoroughly cooked. Save fat in pan.

Ground sausage—Break up as much as possible. Add to a hot pan, reduce heat and cook until light brown, stirring constantly.

If desperate, use patties—Add to a hot pan, cook until desired brown color, turn and cook on the second side. Patties should register at least 150 degrees on a meat thermometer when cooked.

# SAUSAGE & APPLE SOUP

Usually, I make this soup with leftovers a day or so after eating sausage and apples for supper. I add driblets of vegetables at the very end, such as raw English peas and spinach—which wilt in the hot broth—or previously cooked carrots, rice, potatoes, broccoli, and the like.

SERVES 4-6

½ recipe Sausage & Apples (page 52)

1 tablespoon butter

1 medium onion, sliced (about 1 cup)

1 garlic clove, finely chopped

4–6 cups chicken stock or broth

1 cup fresh spinach (optional)

Salt

Black pepper

¾ cup grated cheese, such as Parmesan

Croutons, store-bought or homemade

Prepare the Sausage & Apples by cooking as directed on page 52. When cool, cut into bite-sized pieces.

Melt butter in a large Dutch oven over medium heat. Add onion and stir. Reduce heat to low and cook until very tender and caramelized, about 15 to 20 minutes. Add cooked Sausage & Apples and sauté until warmed through. Add garlic and cook until fragrant, about 1 minute. Stir in 4 cups chicken stock and bring to the boil over medium-high heat to allow the flavors to marry, about 5 minutes, adding more stock if needed. Reduce heat to low and stir in spinach until just wilted. Taste and season with salt and pepper.

To serve, put 1 to 2 tablespoons grated cheese in the bottom of each soup bowl, then ladle soup over the top and garnish with croutons and a little more cheese.

# SAUSAGE & APPLE QUICHE

When I had my restaurant, Nathalie's, in the early '70s in Mount Pleasant Village, Georgia, I started out serving lunches. My friends would frequently drive down from Atlanta to the Hub. It was the era of the quiche. One day at lunch, my friend Leonard mentioned his love of sausage and apple quiche. Immediately after he left, I tested a recipe. I've served it ever since and love it more than the standard bacon and onion quiche.

SERVES 4

½ recipe Sausage & Apples (page 52)

1 recipe Very Versatile Cream Cheese Dough (page 160), or 1 (9-inch) store-bought piecrust

2 tablespoons butter

1 medium shallot, finely chopped (about ¼ cup)

1 garlic clove, finely chopped

½ cup grated cheese such as Comté or cheddar, divided

¾ cup heavy cream

1 whole egg

1 egg yolk

Salt

Freshly ground black pepper

**N O T E :** Frozen pie shells make this dish quick to prepare.

Prepare the Sausage & Apples by cooking as directed on page 52. When cool, cut into bite-sized pieces.

Preheat the oven to 425 degrees. Roll out piecrust and fit into a 9-inch fluted tart pan with a removable bottom. Chill for about 30 minutes. Line with foil or parchment and fill with pie weights, then bake until golden brown and cooked through, about 20 minutes. Allow to cool. Reduce oven temperature to 375 degrees.

Meanwhile, melt the butter in a large skillet over medium heat. Add the shallot and garlic and cook until tender, about 2 to 3 minutes. Remove from heat and stir in chopped Sausage & Apples.

Sprinkle ¼ cup cheese over the bottom of the piecrust. Top with Sausage & Apple mixture.

Mix the cream, egg, and egg yolk together in a small bowl and season with salt and pepper. Pour over the sausage mixture, being careful not to overfill the crust. Top with remaining cheese. Bake until firm in the center, about 20 to 25 minutes. Serve hot or at room temperature.

# SAUSAGE & APPLE OVERNIGHT CASSEROLE

No matter which meal one is eating—breakfast, brunch, lunch, or a breakfast for dinner—this works. Its virtue is being able to be assembled ahead of time and then baked when needed. It's particularly efficient when guests are not sure of their arrival time, or when you take the batter to a weekend gathering and bake it there so it will be hot and welcoming. A salad makes it a meal.

SERVES 12

1 double recipe Sausage & Apples (page 52)

9 large eggs, beaten

2 teaspoons Dijon mustard

3 cups whole milk

1 ½ cups (6 ounces) grated cheese, such as cheddar or Comté

9 slices bread, crusts removed, cut into cubes

Salt

Freshly ground black pepper

Prepare a double recipe of Sausage & Apples as directed on page 52. When cool, cut into bite-sized pieces.

Whisk together eggs, mustard, and milk in a large mixing bowl. Add grated cheese, cubed bread, and cooked Sausage & Apples and stir to combine. Season with salt and pepper. Cover bowl with plastic wrap, or place entire mixture into a large ziplock bag, and refrigerate overnight or up to two days. (If using a bag, fit inside a second bag facing the opposite direction to prevent leakage).

Preheat oven to 350 degrees. Grease a 9 x 13-inch casserole or two 1 ½-quart casseroles. Fill with egg mixture and cover with foil. Bake for 30 minutes covered, then remove foil and bake until golden brown and a knife inserted in the center comes out clean, about another 30 minutes.

# PEANUT BUTTER SANDWICH TO GO

Whenever she wanted to run away—from a job, a man, her children—she made a peanut butter sandwich and thought about the time she'd run away from home with a peanut butter sandwich and a Coke. She had been about ten, a gawky, skinny creature with glasses so thick and strong they reduced her eyes to dark beads.

She thought she didn't have a nice personality and was sure that no one in her family really liked her or had time for her.

Her parents quarreled all the time when they were together. She thought her father was leaving them all soon. He always said he was going to.

It seemed to her it was her fault her parents fought all the time. Maybe if she left—if there would be no one there who was always spilling things or fighting with her brothers and sisters, and if he didn't have her messy room to contend with—maybe then he would stay. She didn't think he liked having any of them, but her least of all. They all said she was the most difficult child.

One day, to her surprise, her dad brought home a bicycle for her. They didn't have a car, so he'd picked it up in the nearby shopping center, thrown his briefcase in the basket, and pedaled the bicycle home on the dusty highway. He had been in high spirits as he pedaled in. Proud of himself in some vain, male way. He was pleased to be able to give her such a present, as nice a bicycle as her friend had.

It had been a happy day. Everyone in the neighborhood had come out to see the bike. She had ridden it some since then, although she was afraid of so much—of leaving it at home, thinking it might not be there when she got back, even if she went to a friend's house for the afternoon.

Later, on the kind of day that was hot when you ran or biked, and cold if you stood still or were in the shadows, she decided to ride away. She spent her life in shadows, it seemed to her—listening to angry words, watching angry scenes, hearing the baby's cries mixed in with her mother's.

She packed her lunch very carefully. She took the store-bought white bread out of the package without making a mess. She spread one slice with peanut butter, then covered it with a second, and cut it in two. She wrapped it in wax paper, and then placed it in the brown bag, along with a banana. She added some gingersnaps from an open box, poured some Coke into her school thermos, and then put the brown bag, all packed, in the basket where her father's briefcase had been so long ago, on a happier day.

Her parents were still shouting when she left the house, and no one asked her where she was going. She knew where she was going.

There was a house a few miles up the highway, a big house, with white columns. She imagined the kind of people who lived there, people with enough money for a car, people who liked little girls, people who would want her.

She pedaled up the hill past her house, looking down on the highway from above, then crossed the road that led to the exit ramp. Cars zoomed past her on the ramp as she pedaled down. Once on the highway itself, there were fewer cars. It was the middle of a hot Saturday, and she was pushing out to the country. She rode a good long while on the flat, even surface before she got hungry. Maybe the white house wasn't as close as she thought. She'd only seen it from the highway. Maybe it wasn't the next exit, maybe it was much farther.

She pulled over onto the dirt strip next to the highway. She peeled open the wrapping around her sandwich and started to eat. It tasted like the banana. She should have known—bananas always give their smell and their flavor. The sandwich was hot and dry and stuck in her throat. She drank some Coke. It was hot, too. The banana had gotten squashed, somehow. Probably by the thermos.

Maybe the people in the house already had children. They probably wouldn't want another. She got back on the bike and pedaled to the next exit. There was no house visible from her side of the highway. She labored up the ramp, ever so tired, and crossed over. There was no house there at all.

She turned back for home, weary and broken in spirit. It was longer going home than it had been leaving, and she had thrown away the rest of her sandwich. She was sorry, and longed for it, even if it tasted like the banana. The rest of the Coke had fizzled out of the thermos and made the cookies soggy and inedible.

It was late when she walked in, and the heat of the day was gone. No one said hello. No one had missed her. She didn't ride her bike much after that. Her dad left soon after and never came home again.

As life went on, she found other foods that comforted her the way peanut butter did and soon she learned that food was not only a way of consoling herself but of nurturing others. When she moved to another country, she served American meat loaf, macaroni, and greens to her exiled friends. When she was left alone, she cooked onions to comfort her in her loneliness. And always, she kept gingersnaps on hand and a jar of peanut butter. All of them, when she needed them, soothed and comforted her.

# MAIN COURSES

These are my important main courses. As a rule they can serve more than two, with most of them able to be served to anyone at anytime. The last few—the Southern Bouillabaisse and the Cassoulet, among others—are suited for more than just a few, and they take thought and time, although each of the steps is easy and nothing is foreboding except the number of ingredients.

I've included roast chickens and turkey because I think everyone should learn to cook them. Due to their shape and having both light and dark meat, they don't cook evenly; but once understood, they can just be thrown into the oven with their seasonings and left alone most of the time. Their flavor outshines that of any other simple dish, and they provide leftovers.

I live on the seacoast, so fish also play a prominent role in my life, after going most of my life with only a favored few and rarely having just-caught seafood. What a pleasure they are.

Note: If you are missing shrimp and grits in this section, because it is so easily an evening meal, you will find it in breakfasts.

GARLIC-STUFFED ROAST CHICKEN

69

GRILLED ROMAN-STYLE LEMON CHICKEN

70

FENNEL-OLIVE RELISH

73

TURKEY WITH GRAVY

79

TRADITIONAL TURKEY GRAVY

81

AMBER TURKEY STOCK

84

CYNTHIA'S GRILLED BEEF TENDERLOIN

86

BEEF TENDERLOIN STUFFED WITH
MUSHROOM & SPINACH DUXELLES

89

ROMESCO SAUCE

91

# HOME-COOKED MEALS

My 105-pound, very attractive friend arrived having had a couple of drinks. "Can I fix you some dinner?" I asked, being a bit hungry myself and ready for real food. "No," she said, "I'm being good. Last night I ate a great chocolate dessert at the restaurant!" As if not eating dinner was being good. Since when did being good have anything to do with dinner?

This whole fad of not eating at home and going on a binge in a restaurant undermines the fundamental joy of food. Food should be nurturing, a means of sharing with friends and family at home, and creating bridges for communication and exchanging memories. What a switch from when I was a child and you had to eat what was in front of you, whether you wanted it or not. If you weren't punished for not eating all your food, you were at least made to feel guilty about all the starving children in China who didn't have enough to eat—as if that food from your plate could mysteriously have been delivered to a child in China. And you didn't get dessert if you didn't eat the main course. Surely, somewhere in between there is a sensible balance.

Another dear friend is very worried about her husband's cholesterol. Once every couple of months I have a craving for country-cooked greasy foods, which I satisfy at home. The other day, she joined us when we were eating a lunch of turnip greens and cornbread made with fatback.

She declared how good it was and how much her husband would love it. "Don't you fix turnip greens for him any more?" we asked. "NO!" she said. "I keep him on a strict diet. But he goes out three times a week with his cronies, and that's when they eat all this rich, fattening food." We asked if fixing it occasionally at home—enough to satisfy his cravings for what was familiar—would stop him from eating incorrectly those three times a week. "NO," she said, "he wants it when he goes out to eat."

What a shame! The food that satisfies him, makes him happy, makes him feel nurtured, is what he gets away from home. What he eats at home is tasty—she's a good cook. Her efforts in her own kitchen at home have reduced his cholesterol, and he is now in good physical shape. But they have decided between them that the restaurant is the place for special occasions for him, and home is the place for what he feels is punishment food—the healthy food. She can feel good about keeping him healthy, because she doesn't actually feed him or see him eating the food she knows is bad for him. Thus he can "sin" out of the home with his fat-laden meals.

I have another friend, whom I call a cook-on-a-perch since he doesn't cook every day, as I do. He mostly eats out. He complains about my using canned chicken stock in an everyday soup. Dilettante cook that he is, he can look down his nose at those of us who feed family and friends day in and day out, and say, "No canned chicken stock, pul-leeze. It is too salty." When salty canned stock is reduced by boiling, it can be too salty. But when it is simmered gently and briefly, or diluted, it is not. More importantly, it is much better than no stock at all in the soup, or eating out. Moreover, the number of restaurants that use homemade chicken stock is very small—all but the finest use a prepared product!

This same man who complains about the salt in my canned chicken stock knows which brand of potato chips are his favorite and is a connoisseur of beers. It isn't salt he objects to—it is salt on real food. I know people who eat high-salt frozen foods that are low in calories (promoted as being "slim" or "lean" foods) but that are also often high in cholesterol or additives. My potato-chip friend also loves ice cream.

The egg is currently getting a bad rap from the cholesterol-conscious. Yet while the simple egg is still the best form of nutrition for a starving family, many low-income families don't know how to cook an egg and frequently spend much too great a proportion of their income on so-called fast foods and eating out. They'd rather have a fatty hamburger any day than eat an egg at home.

A solution? I don't have one that everyone will accept. I am for balanced meals and for not overeating any one thing. Unless your medical doctor has put you on a special diet, I'm for having meat loaf and mashed potatoes one night, and grilled chicken and steamed vegetables the next. I'm for eating at home and serving a meal that satisfies as well as nourishes. And, if "sin" is the issue, let it be chocolate—the whole family does deserve an occasional chocolate bash!

# GARLIC-STUFFED ROAST CHICKEN

When I was chef of the restaurant C'an Poleta in Majorca, the only cookbooks I had were one by Michael Fields and the Cordon Bleu paperback I had used in cooking school. This recipe, adapted from Michael Fields, is actually a much older one, its origins in French cookery long ago. It has kept its popularity over the ages because it is so delicious. The garlic melts as it cooks and its flavor changes to a gentler one than when raw.

SERVES 4 TO 6

2 tablespoons oil, cook's preference

2 tablespoons butter

50 garlic cloves, peeled

1 (3-pound) whole chicken

2 sprigs fresh rosemary, more for serving if desired

2 cups chicken stock, divided

Salt

Freshly ground black pepper

Preheat oven to 425 degrees.

Heat the oil and butter over medium heat in a large frying pan. Add the 50 garlic cloves and cook for a few minutes, until slightly brown. Remove garlic with a slotted spoon, shaking off excess fat, and stuff inside the chicken cavity with the rosemary sprigs. Brush the outside with any remaining oil and butter from the pan.

Move the chicken into a metal or ovenproof roasting pan and tie the legs together or truss. Add ½ cup chicken stock to the pan. Bake until the thickest part of the chicken reaches 165-170 degrees on an instant-read thermometer, about 45 minutes to 1 hour, turning over once.

Remove the chicken and set aside. Add remaining broth to the pan. Spoon out the garlic from the chicken and add to the pan. Bring to the boil and boil steadily until liquid reduces by half. Skim off fat. Taste and season with salt and pepper. Serve chicken with the sauce. May be made ahead 1 to 2 days and reheated, but it's best served freshly made.

T i p :  To peel a large quantity of garlic cloves, find two metal bowls of the same size. Separate cloves into one bowl and cover with the other like a dome. Holding the two bowls together tightly, shake several times until peel comes off easily.

# GRILLED ROMAN-STYLE LEMON CHICKEN

There was a time when Marcella Hazan and a few others brought Italian cooking to America. It is hard to separate the recipes from the cooking we all did because those recipes are as familiar to us as our own. Marcella conducted cooking classes in Italy attended by worshipful acolytes, although I did not learn this recipe from her. I learned it around the same time but first tasted it with a group of food writers on the roof top of a simple restaurant. I came home and cooked and taught it at Rich's cooking school. That recipe is lost to the years, as sometimes I stuff lemon slices under the skin and sometimes cook it as is. But when in doubt, I double check Marcella's books.

SERVES 4 TO 6

1 (3-pound) whole chicken

½–¾ cup lemon juice

2 tablespoons lemon zest

4 tablespoons oil, cook's preference, divided

Salt

Freshly ground black pepper

1 lemon, sliced, for garnish

With the chicken breast facing down, remove the backbone by cutting up either side of the backbone with a sharp knife or kitchen scissors. Flip the chicken over with its breast on top. Crack the breastbone using both your hands and spread the chicken as flat as possible. Use a small knife to make small vertical slits where the wings and legs join the body, without removing them, in order to flatten it. Turn the chicken over and lay a sheet of plastic wrap over the top. Using a meat pounder or the bottom side of a heavy skillet, pound it out as flat as possible. Remove plastic.

Move the chicken to a large ziplock bag or roasting pan. Mix lemon juice, lemon zest, and 2 tablespoons of the oil together in a small bowl and pour over the chicken. Season with salt and pepper. Close bag or cover pan and refrigerate for 2 to 3 hours to marinate. Remove from refrigerator about 30 minutes before ready to cook.

Preheat the oven to 500 degrees.

> CONTINUED

Preheat a flat, oven-proof grill or griddle pan on top of the stove over medium heat. Remove chicken to a paper towel-lined plate, drain marinade into a small saucepan, and set aside. Pat chicken dry.

Wrap a heavy ovenproof skillet or a brick with aluminum foil. Add the remaining 2 tablespoons oil to the hot pan, then the chicken, skin-side down. Weigh down with the heavy skillet. Brown over medium heat, about 5 minutes. Carefully move to the hot oven with the weight on top. Cook 10 minutes. Meanwhile, bring the marinade to the boil and boil a few minutes. Remove the weight from the chicken. Brush the chicken with reserved marinade and flip chicken over. Cook until chicken reaches an internal temperature of 165 degrees on an instant-read thermometer, about 10 to 15 minutes.

When chicken is done, move to a board to rest. Brown the lemon slices lightly in the pan juices, about 4 to 5 minutes. Garnish chicken with the sliced lemons. Add any remaining pan juices to the reserved marinade. Serve the cooked marinade and Fennel-Olive Relish (page 73) alongside the chicken.

# FENNEL-OLIVE RELISH

The first person who thought of combining fennel and olives deserves a rush of praise, and so I praise this for its ever tastiness. It goes with almost anything savory and is a favorite of mine above pickle-type relishes. I got the original recipe from David Tanis in the *New York Times* but have adapted and changed it. I've been making it for so long that it's a bit slap dash in the making.

I use a food processor, which makes quick work of the recipe and results in a tapenade-like texture. For a more rustic finish, the ingredients can be finely chopped by hand. If chopping the parsley in the food processor, use an empty, dry food processor bowl. Chop the parsley first and then set it aside in a prep dish.

MAKES 1 ½ CUPS

2 garlic cloves

1 ½ cups pitted black olives

½ fennel bulb, root and stems, with fronds removed and reserved

1 teaspoon lemon zest, no white included

1–2 tablespoons lemon juice

Freshly ground black pepper

1 tablespoon chopped fresh parsley

1 tablespoon finely chopped fennel fronds

2 tablespoons chopped capers, optional

Add garlic to the bowl of a food processor fitted with the metal blade and pulse until finely chopped. Add olives and pulse a few times until chopped. Thinly slice fennel and add to food processor; pulse until evenly chopped, 4 to 5 times. Remove to a bowl, and add lemon zest and lemon juice. Season with black pepper. Chop the fennel fronds. Stir in the parsley and chopped fennel fronds. Add capers, if using. It will last in a container refrigerated for a week.

# HEROINE'S FEAST

In the way that foods have of becoming fashionable, pigeon is now in vogue. Sometimes it is called squab, which is really a baby pigeon.

My first experience in cooking pigeons was with my Uncle Ray. As my mother liked to remind us, Uncle Ray was only an uncle by marriage. The implication was that he did things that our family would not do. One of them was to catch pigeons on the railroad trestle. He had done this since he was a small boy, bringing them home to his mother for supper. As a grown man, he relished the memory of his mother's squabs and wanted his wife—my Aunt Marion—to bring back for him the magic of his mother's cooking by cooking the pigeons he brought home. My Aunt Marion was not the best of cooks although she made a wonderful Kool-Aid punch full of fresh fruit, and a great sliced ham sandwich. But she did not like cooking those pigeons.

Each summer when we went to visit my grandmother and aunt, we would go out with Uncle Ray to catch the squabs. My sister and I would be roused from our beds early in the morning to pile into the car, the sleep barely washed from our eyes. We wore what girls wore in those days—cotton pants, a halter, and a cotton long-sleeve shirt.

Ray's railroad trestle (our abiding name for it, although it belonged, clearly, to the railroad company) was over a big body of water, perhaps a rushing stream, and stretched a considerable distance. It was wooden, with gravel and stones between the tracks. Uncle Ray would park the old car at the bottom of a very steep embankment, which we would then climb up with nothing to hold onto except scrubby grass and dirt and an occasional scrawny tree.

Each of us would carry shoe boxes under our arms with holes punched by a screwdriver, in which we would place our prey. We would also bring some tape to hold the lid down as we slipped and slid down the hill with our quarry.

Once on top of the trestle, we would walk the tracks looking for the birds. They had to be exactly the right size to suit Ray, who knew just what he wanted. Whenever he had settled for large pigeons he had been disappointed. We were looking for little pigeons he could take home, fatten up and clean out for a few days, and then get my aunt to kill in some unspeakable manner and to roast them. We liked the idea of garnering the squabs, bringing them home to my Aunt Marion, and having them to play with for some days. We liked neither the killing nor the eating of them.

Neither did Aunt Marion, who found keeping the squabs on the side porch a dirty, nasty process, and who muttered constantly about the fact that pigeons were filthy birds—as anyone could tell by going down to the Capitol and seeing the mess they made.

The last time my Aunt Marion let us go squab hunting was when a train came over the tracks. One thing Uncle Ray had always neglected to tell Aunt Marion was that there were a lot of KEEP OFF signs on the trestle. There was no room on the trestle for anything but a train. What railings there were weren't suitable for hanging on to. So, when the train came, there was general confusion. Fortunately, we had heard the sound of the train from a distance.

This time we were in the middle of the narrow trestle. We had filled our boxes with some plump little birds and were sitting with our feet dangling over the side, looking at the water, basking in the sun, when suddenly we heard the sound of the train. There was no whistle. Maybe trains don't whistle on bridges that are supposed to be empty. But we heard the chugging and looked up to see it heading right for us. We grabbed our boxes, leaving behind our shirts, running all the while to the end of the trestle.

Uncle Ray was a coward to boot. Running ahead of us, he yelled back to us to hurry. We were running as hard as we could, unthinkingly clutching those shoe boxes. At the end of the trestle, which he reached way before we did, he found an insecure perch on the side of the steep hill and grabbed for us. By then the conductor had spotted us, and the train was whistling loud and clear. But, of course, the train couldn't stop, and we had the good sense to know that seeing us and stopping the train were two different things.

We made it. We got some cuts and scratches as we scrambled down the hill with our boxes wedged under our arms. I had slipped on the gravel and had some fragments embedded in my arm. We washed in the stream as best we could, but it didn't clean us up much. We had lost our shirts as well as tearing our pants. When we got home, we were all scolded, including Uncle Ray.

Before we left that summer, we ate those birds. In spite of my Aunt's grumbling that we could have all been killed, Uncle Ray persisted in feeding them and, finally, "putting them to rest." Aunt Marion browned them and set them in a pan in the oven and finished them off. They were delicious, fat, moist. For some reason I didn't mind eating those squabs. Maybe because by then I had embellished the story of my near-death so that in my mind it was a heroine's feast.

# TURKEY WITH GRAVY

Brining seems to be a necessary evil for the mass-produced turkey. Organic ones, however, seem to be fine without it, or with just a light rub of salt.

For many of us, carving a turkey at the table is a needlessly difficult task contrived by Norman Rockwell and Charles Dickens; I feel it should be done in the kitchen. Rather than stuff the turkey, which contributes to a dry breast, flavor it with an onion, carrot, and a few fresh herbs placed in the cavity. Sometimes a quartered lemon. If a rack is not available, the onions and carrots can form a resting place for the turkey in the bottom of the roasting pan. I keep stock in the bottom of the pan to prevent burning of the juices and ensure a scrumptious gravy. This creates a bit of steam, so take care when opening and closing the oven.

SERVES 8 TO 10

| | |
|---|---|
| 1 (12-to-14-pound) turkey, fresh or thawed | Salt |
| Oil for pan | Freshly ground black pepper |
| 3 onions, quartered, divided | ½–1 cup heavy cream, optional |
| 3 carrots, divided | **BASTING LIQUID**, optional |
| 1 lemon, quartered, optional | 1 cup white wine |
| Chopped fresh herbs to taste, such as rosemary, sage, thyme, optional | ½ cup butter |
| | 1 sprig thyme |
| ½ cup melted butter or oil, cook's preference | 1 sprig sage |
| 4–6 cups turkey or chicken stock or broth | 1 bay leaf |

Preheat oven to 450 degrees. Have a large piece of cheesecloth at hand.

Defrost turkey, if frozen, in the refrigerator, which may take several days. Unwrap fresh or frozen turkey a day or several hours ahead in the refrigerator to dry the skin. Oil a large roasting pan and rack, if using, and set aside (I use a giant, round, flat-bottomed roasting pan, similar to a deep paella pan).

Clean the turkey of any parts at the neck or the cavity. Add half the onions and carrots and all the lemon, if using, with the fresh herbs to the cavity of the turkey. If using a rack, put the remaining vegetables underneath in the roasting pan. If not, put the carrots in the center of the pan, with the onions surrounding them.

> CONTINUED

Tie the turkey's legs together and move to the rack or on top of the vegetables in the prepared pan. Brush turkey with butter or oil, particularly the breast. Add enough stock to come 1 to 2 inches up the sides of the turkey. Roast for 1 hour.

Open the door carefully to remove turkey from the oven, watching out for steam. If the stock has boiled down to less than 1 inch up the sides, add enough to bring it up to 2 inches. Return it to the oven and roast for 1 hour more. Cover with foil if browning too much. Or make the optional Basting Liquid by combining all ingredients in a small pot and bringing to the boil. Reduce heat to low and simmer a few minutes to allow herbs to infuse their flavor; then remove from heat. Carefully dip the cheesecloth into the warm mixture just to moisten, then lay across the top of the turkey. Continue cooking the turkey, basting occasionally with remaining liquid.

Remove the turkey and check for doneness. An instant-read thermometer inserted in the thigh should read 165 degrees, and the juices should run clear when a knife is inserted into the flesh of the thigh. Remove and let rest 30 minutes before carving. There will be some wonderful pan juices. If the juices seem fatty, skim off the fat with a paper towel or use a fat separator (see Degreasing, page 85). Add any remaining stock to the pan. Move pan to a burner and bring juices to the boil over high heat, stirring constantly, and boil down to reduce until rich and flavorful. Season to taste with salt and pepper. Use the juices alone as a light sauce, or make traditional gravy (page 81). For a richer sauce, add the cream and boil until thick.

# NOTES

- A good instant-read thermometer is a must for judging accurately when a turkey is done.

- Rubbing a turkey, frozen or defrosted, with 1 tablespoon salt per 5 pounds of turkey 2 or 3 days in advance and massaging a couple of times a day will result in a tastier turkey and allow osmosis to occur, tenderizing the meat. Pat dry with a paper towel. In addition, leaving the turkey an hour or so at room temperature before baking and allowing the skin to dry out a bit will result in a crisper skin.

- It is easier for me to roast two smaller turkeys than one larger one. My reasoning is that a large turkey takes longer to cook, is more challenging for the home cook to handle, and is difficult to store before cooking. Using two small turkeys allows for one of them to be roasted and carved ahead of time, even the night before, and one to be the "show piece" on the table. The carved turkey takes up less space in the refrigerator, and there are all those wonderful bones for stock, gravy, and soup.

# TRADITIONAL TURKEY GRAVY

Gravy is the star of the turkey. My grandmother always made the gravy at my Aunt Flo's Thanksgiving dinners. Everyone bragged on it while poor Flo got no credit for doing everything else.

Making gravy at the last minute is maddening and unnecessary. Make the gravy the night before Thanksgiving from the juices of the extra turkey (page 80), or from previously made stock. Keep it refrigerated covered, and reheat it in the microwave. If there aren't enough juices, boil up some of those extra turkey bones to make additional stock. See the Amber Turkey Stock recipe (page 84) if an additional turkey is not available, and make it ahead so that there will be sufficient stock to make enough gravy. Both stock and gravy freeze well. Remember the liver is to be used for another purpose as it makes the gravy bitter.

MAKES 4 CUPS

3 tablespoons fat from the pan juices

Giblets, cut up, optional

4 tablespoons all-purpose flour

2–3 cups turkey or chicken stock or broth, degreased, see page 85

1 cup heavy cream, optional, divided

Salt

Freshly ground black pepper

Heat 3 tablespoons of the fat over high heat in a 2-quart saucepan. Add the giblets if using, without the liver, and brown. Whisking continuously, add the flour and cook until the mixture turns light brown, about 2 to 3 minutes, making a roux. Whisk in the stock, and continue to stir or whisk until boiling and thickened. If it is lumpy, strain it and return to the pan. If using the cream, add half to the hot pan and whisk over heat until thickened and reduced. (It is okay to boil the cream, provided the pan is a sufficient size to hold stock and cream.) Taste and add more cream if desired, return to the boil, and boil until reduced slightly. Season to taste with salt and pepper. Cover with plastic wrap to prevent a skin from forming on the top of the gravy. Refrigerate up to 3 days or freeze. Reheat in microwave or on stovetop.

# GIVING THANKS

Thanksgiving is a holiday in which food takes on the leading role. There is perhaps no other day in America when the entire activity rests on feeding and eating. Yet it is also fraught with hidden agendas and mixed feelings. In addition to the joy of being with family and friends, tensions can develop that stretch the full length of the table. The pressure on the cook, as well as the diner, is enormous, and the power exchanges mighty. Let's assume that there is great love and affection at the meal. But as relationships change, there are issues in a family that need to be negotiated and understood. Sometimes these are unspoken, but they are still there.

Learning how to negotiate and to be flexible in feeding others on this day brings food into its seat of power. Who, for instance, when agendas are mixed, determines the time of eating? Will the meal interfere with a football game, a date, or perhaps a commitment to another set of family, such as in-laws? Why, on this one day of all days, should people who normally eat at twelve or one and then again at seven or eight be hungry at three or five? A wise cook focuses the fete as close to a normal eating time as possible, and makes provisions for her guests clear when making arrangements. Tummies and tempers will be better for it. Providing a snack if the meal is to be delayed will help.

The cook is subject to a set of skewed feelings. Will she or he feel obligated to rise early and give up the greater portion of a day (or days) to work the serving time around people who would rather be elsewhere? Does the cook feel that if the meal isn't eaten with gusto at a certain time it is evidence of lack of appreciation? And will she or he have time to clean up, alone, while everyone flees to another activity?

I can rarely be gracious about delayed meals (in my home or others') when others don't want to give up another activity to come to the table, or because they think the time of eating is not crucial.

The guest list is important—to everyone. Fantasies on one person's part of inviting the homeless or great aunt, but counting on others to entertain them, can cause family upheaval. At the same time, omitting a favorite aunt or girl friend of a teenager, or not figuring out a way to include in-laws or the needy may make someone feel a real sense of loss at an otherwise happy time.

Some people like strangers, others don't. I'll never forget the time I spontaneously invited a stranger in town to an in-law's table, thinking I had checked and understood. I didn't.

Expectations of the diners become a force as well. Do they expect someone who never cooks for more than four all year long to all of a sudden be able to prepare dinner for fifteen with no help? Is their idea of the holiday to just show up and be fed? Has the cook prepared a way for them to help?

Hopefully, we are beyond the days of one person feeling that she or he has to do it all. It's not realistic. But there are still people who sense a loss of control if others help, and there are still eaters who feel they have no responsibility to others or themselves for their pleasure at table.

Some of them don't even think they should express thanks. They are the greatest losers, for by not expressing their gratitude, they give up the acknowledgment of the good in their lives. What a good holiday meal for everyone means is finding a way to understand each other's needs and to give a little—time, companionship, help—to make everyone feel loved. This is the way we will learn to feed the world.

# AMBER TURKEY STOCK

This is my favorite stock. Browned turkey wings and neck pieces provide a good base, resulting in a full-flavored stock that is more practical for me than chicken stock, but I use both. At holiday time, I always make a stock from browned wings and necks. I cool and then freeze it for later. The browned bones and flesh produce a beautiful amber-colored stock. It is very useful for extra gravy, dressings, and soups. Gravy made from turkey stock is substantially earthier and more succulent than chicken or many other stocks. The more the bones are chopped, the more natural gelatin will be in the stock.

MAKES 2 QUARTS

3 pounds turkey wings, backs, necks, or other pieces

1 medium onion, thickly sliced, including brown peel

1 large carrot, thickly sliced

1 celery rib, thickly sliced, optional

3–4 parsley stalks, optional

1/4 cup mushroom stems, optional

6 black peppercorns, optional

1 bay leaf

1/4 teaspoon dried thyme

Preheat oven to 350 degrees.

Using a meat cleaver, chop the turkey meat and bones into smaller pieces. Move the turkey pieces, onion, carrot, and optional ingredients to a heavy rimmed baking sheet and into the oven. Roast, turning occasionally. Smaller pieces will brown more quickly, so remove them as they turn a very dark brown with perhaps a small touch of black. This will take approximately 30 to 45 minutes.

Move the turkey bones and meat and all other ingredients to a deep stockpot or saucepan. Add bay leaf and thyme. Add 1/2 cup water to the roasting pan. Bring to the boil over medium heat, deglazing the pan (scraping brown bits from the bottom and sides; it's also a good way to clean the pan). Pour into the pot of bones and meat, along with enough water to cover the ingredients. Bring to the boil over high heat then reduce the heat to low and simmer for about 2 hours, adding water as needed to keep the wings covered.

Strain the stock through a fine mesh strainer or a colander lined with dampened cheesecloth, pressing the solids to release all of the juices and extract their flavor. Cool the stock and refrigerate several hours or overnight. When cold, skim off all the fat that has risen to the surface. The stock can be refrigerated up to 3 days, or it can be frozen, using containers of a size that will accommodate future needs, such as 1-quart freezer bags or containers.

## DEGREASING

There are a number of ways to remove fat formed on the top of food:

• While cooking, move the pan and tilt it slightly to allow all the fat and any scum to gather together at one place, making it easier to skim or spoon off.

• Run strips of paper towel over the top of the liquid. The fat on top will come off with the towel.

• Hold an ice cube and slide it over the top of the liquid. The fat will congeal on the outside of the cube.

• Use a special cup with a pouring spout located near the bottom of the cup; the fat will remain in the cup as the degreased portion of the sauce is poured out.

• Chill. The fat will come to the top and congeal, ready to be scooped off.

# CYNTHIA'S GRILLED BEEF TENDERLOIN

Tenderloin is miraculous in its expansiveness. It is lovely roasted whole and then sliced thickly as a main course for a sit-down meal. Or, for a cocktail party, split in half lengthwise before roasting, and sliced thinly to serve with small rolls. I've had people stand around the platter sopping up the juices with the extra rolls. That's okay, too. It's named after Cynthia because it is what I cooked for her and Cliff's engagement supper. It was an early summer evening with just the right weather, as well as a pool reflecting the lights and a full moon. It was a perfect night—just what every bride wants for that special party.

SERVES 8 TO 10, OR 20 TO 25 AT A BUFFET

1 beef tenderloin (about 3 ½–5 pounds), stripped of silver skin, fat, and gristle, and chain removed

2 cups low sodium soy sauce or tamari

2/3 cup dark sesame oil

6 large garlic cloves, chopped

2 tablespoons chopped fresh ginger

Move the tenderloin to a ziplock plastic bag or container. Whisk together the soy sauce, oil, garlic, and ginger, and pour half of the marinade over the tenderloin. (If using a bag, fit inside a second bag facing the opposite direction to prevent leakage). Reserve the remaining marinade for the sauce in a separate container. Marinate the beef in the container in the refrigerator. Marinating for 1 hour is sufficient if you are in a rush, but I frequently marinate this overnight, or at least by morning for serving that evening. Much longer, however, will not help and will perhaps make the meat too soft.

Prepare a charcoal grill, if using, or preheat oven to 425 degrees.

Remove the tenderloin from the refrigerator 1 hour before cooking. Move to a preheated charcoal grill over low fire, covered, or place on a foil-lined roasting pan in the preheated oven. Cook, turning occasionally to brown all over, until the meat registers 125 degrees on an instant-read thermometer inserted into the thickest part of the tenderloin, about 30-45 minutes depending on thickness. Remove from heat and let rest before serving.

While the meat rests, add the reserved marinade to the pan drippings and bring to the boil, scraping the pan. Remove any excess fat. Slice meat and serve with sauce. The tenderloin may be roasted ahead and reheated. Serve hot or cold.

# TENDERLOIN

Tenderloin is sold both untrimmed and trimmed and peeled. The average untrimmed beef tenderloin is 7 to 9 pounds, including the butt and ¾ inches of fat and membrane as well as the "chain." One third of the weight is lost when fat and chain are removed. Peeled tenders originally weigh 5 to 7 pounds and are then sold trimmed at 3 ½ to 4 pounds. There is very little price savings when buying trimmed (peeled) vs. untrimmed tenderloin when all calculations are finished, so buy the best thing for convenience. The difference in size of tenderloins and the unknown amount of fat (some are also sold partially trimmed) makes it difficult to do a price comparison. If possible, get the butcher to trim it; be sure, however, to ask for the chain.

# BEEF TENDERLOIN STUFFED WITH MUSHROOM & SPINACH DUXELLES

A tenderloin brings a lot to the table, even though it is an expensive cut of meat because it can serve a crowd and become as expansive as a less expensive cut. It can be served thick or thin for a posh dinner party, a casual outdoor buffet, or for rolls at a cocktail party. Tenderloin is indestructible unless overcooked and even then is salvageable. Stuffed, it brings cachet. A good meat thermometer relieves much of the anxiety surrounding cooking an expensive cut of meat. Serve this tenderloin with either Romesco Sauce (pictured) (page 91), or with Aïoli (page 104) if desired.

SERVES 8 TO 10, OR 20 TO 25 AT A BUFFET

1 beef tenderloin (about 3 ½–5 pounds), stripped of silver skin, fat, and gristle, and chain removed

Freshly ground black pepper

1 recipe Duxelles, below

2 tablespoons oil, cook's preference, divided

Romesco Sauce, optional (page 91)

Duxelles:

1 pint grape tomatoes, halved

1 tablespoon oil, cook's preference

Salt

Freshly ground black pepper

2 garlic cloves

8 ounces fresh mushrooms, such as shiitake or cremini, tough stems removed

4 tablespoons butter

½ cup finely chopped shallots (from 2 large or 4 small shallots)

4 cups fresh spinach, chopped, or 5 ounces frozen chopped spinach, defrosted and well drained

¾ cup grated Comté cheese

Preheat oven to 425 degrees.

Prepare the meat for stuffing by opening it up. If the tenderloin still has the "butt" end attached, use a long sharp knife and follow the line of fat to separate the butt from the rest of the tenderloin (there is a "line" of fat in the meat that is easy to follow). This can be rolled and roasted alongside the tenderloin. Prepare the remaining as follows: Cut the tenderloin lengthwise down the center, leaving a hinge in the middle so as to open like a book. With the knife parallel to the cutting board, slice the meat carefully in half from the middle of the meat out toward to the side, again leaving a hinge. Repeat on the

> CONTINUED

opposite side. Now there are three parallel hinges making one wide piece of meat. Cover with plastic wrap and pound to become a uniform piece of meat about 1 inch thick.

To make Duxelles, toss tomatoes with 1 tablespoon oil and season with salt and pepper. Roast in pre-heated oven until soft, about 8 minutes. Remove and allow to cool.

Chop the garlic and mushrooms in the bowl of a food processor fitted with the metal blade. Pulse until very finely chopped. Melt the butter in a large skillet. Add shallots and cook until soft, 2 to 3 minutes. Add mushroom mixture and cook until all the liquid has evaporated and mushrooms are tender, about 8 minutes. Add chopped spinach and allow to wilt, stirring until evenly combined. Transfer to a bowl and allow to cool. Stir in cheese and cooled tomatoes.

Cover the open meat with an even layer of the duxelles mixture. Roll the beef, starting from one side and continuing to the other. Tie securely with butcher's twine. This can be done up to 24 hours in advance.

When ready to cook, bring to room temperature and rub with 2 tablespoons oil. Move the meat to a roasting pan and cook in preheated oven until a meat thermometer registers 125-130 degrees, about 30 to 45 minutes. Season immediately with salt and pepper. If serving hot, remove and let sit 10 minutes before slicing to desired thickness. If serving cold, refrigerating before slicing makes the slicing easier.

# ROMESCO SAUCE

This is a sauce I made frequently in Majorca and always thought it was from there, only to find out that it is Mediterranean and usually thought to be Italian. Anyplace with abundant almonds can claim it, serving it with meat, fish, or vegetables or stirring a bit into soups, stews, and even vegetables.

MAKES 2 CUPS

3 red bell peppers (or substitute jarred roasted red peppers)

½ cup whole almonds

4–5 garlic cloves

½ cup panko breadcrumbs

1 tablespoon sherry vinegar

Salt

¼–⅓ cup extra virgin olive oil

Roast the red bell peppers on the grill or under the broiler, very close to the heat, turning often until charred all over, nearly black. Remove and place in a plastic bag to steam off skin. When cool enough to handle, remove charred skin and seed the peppers. (If using jarred roasted peppers, skip to the next step.)

Toast the almonds in a dry skillet over medium-low heat until golden; watch carefully so as not to burn them. Remove to a bowl. Add whole garlic cloves to the skillet and toast until lightly golden brown.

Place roasted peppers, almonds, garlic, panko, sherry vinegar, and a pinch of salt in the bowl of a food processor fitted with the metal blade. Purée 60 to 90 seconds, until well combined. With the motor running, slowly stream in the olive oil until it is emulsified and a sauce consistency forms, though it will not get completely smooth. Taste and adjust seasoning if necessary. Cover and chill at least 30 minutes before serving to allow the flavors to marry.

# GRANDMOTHER'S POT ROAST

When I think of Republicans, I think of my grandmother's pot roast sandwiches at the time of the great 1952 Republican National Convention, when my grandmother had come to stay with us. A devout religious woman who knew God was not an old man in the sky, she nonetheless could not shake the opinion that God was a Republican.

Grandmother was so riveted by politics and news that the television was on all the time, day and night. Our new television was enshrined in the middle of the living room, and for the first time we were allowed to not only eat in front of the television but also stay up later than our bedtime to watch the convention.

The morning of the nomination for the Republican candidate, she got up in the cool of the morning and put on the pot roast, turning and browning it in hot fat. The night before (a hot night that was also a late night for television), she had started some homemade bread, leaving it to rise in the cool basement. She knocked it down and shaped it, letting it double again as the meat was browning, and then baked it. The smell of baking bread was added to the tantalizing smells of cooking meat when we came down for our oatmeal.

Grandmother was a wizard with the lowly potato and boiled up a batch of them, some to be put in to finish with the juices of the pot roast, some for later. All day we sniffed that meat and the lingering smell of baked bread emanating from the loaves put out to cool on the racks in the tiny kitchen.

She called her candidate "Mr. Republican." He was Senator Robert Taft, the son of the 27th President of the United States, William Howard Taft. He was in contention for the nomination against General Dwight D. Eisenhower, who had flirted briefly with the Democrats and wasn't even, to my grandmother's way of thinking, a Republican for sure.

My grandmother had supported Taft for three elections. He ran for president in 1940, 1948, and 1952, losing each time. She hated Thomas Dewey, his opponent in 1948, as much as she had hated Franklin Delano Roosevelt — and she was so convinced of the rightness and reason of the Republican party's political stance that she couldn't even bear the names of the Democrats. I vaguely remember as a younger child watching a parade or commemorative service for the dead president Franklin Delano Roosevelt, but I didn't understand the politics. I thought they were saying a rose was dead, and I started to cry. My grandmother yanked my hand and pulled me away from the scene of activity, sniffing, "Pretty names don't make pretty people." She also said that Truman's name was a lie—he wasn't a "true man." A Democrat could do no good.

The convention of 1952 was a spellbinder. We sat in front of that television until long into the night, watching the black-and-white figures parade up and down, hearing the state roll calls, and keeping count on a sheet provided by the newspaper so you could tally up the votes. It was endless—and tense. The world was watching. Sometime during the night, we ate thick sandwiches of pot roast and slices of buttered bread and drank Grandmother's famous iced tea. We were engrossed with the drama and power of a televised convention played out in front of our eyes. We became part of the ground of politics.

It was hot, beastly hot, I remember. We had no air conditioners then—did anyone?—and the screened windows and doors were wide open. Finally, at the end, General Eisenhower, to Grandmother's indignation, won a narrow victory over Taft, and my grandmother knew her candidate would never be president.

She knew she couldn't sleep, between the heat and her sorrow. Nor could we, hyper with the activity long past our bedtime. She took cold potatoes and sliced them, making us a potato sandwich with the fresh bread, using plenty of salt and pepper. Then she took our sheets and pillows out to the front lawn and spread them out. We lay under the stars and ate our picnic sandwiches as she talked to us about the rightness of the world and God's sorrow with the Republicans. At dawn she woke us so the neighbors wouldn't see us camping out, and made us breakfast of bread dipped in sugar and milk.

# LEMON-LIME POT ROAST WITH TOMATOES & GARLIC

When we made this while taping the TV series at Georgia Public TV, the all-male crew oohed and aahed. Unfortunately, we spilled the leftover sauce onto the floor as we cleared the set. It took the top layer of the stain off the cement floor. So be judicious about the amount of the citrus juices; size matters, even with lemons and limes.

SERVES 4 TO 6

1 (2- to- 3-pound) chuck, round, or sirloin tip roast

4 garlic cloves, chopped

Grated rind and juice of 2 or 3 limes, no white attached, divided

Grated rind and juice of 2 lemons, no white attached, divided

4 tablespoons bacon fat or drippings, or oil, cook's preference

1 ½ cups beef stock or broth

1 (14 ½-ounce) can diced tomatoes with juice

Pinch of sugar, optional

1–2 tablespoons chopped fresh rosemary

1–3 tablespoons chopped marjoram, lemon thyme, or other fresh herbs, optional

Salt

Freshly ground black pepper

Remove any tough pieces of fat or sinew from the roast.

Mash the garlic together with 1 tablespoon of each of the grated rinds and rub over the meat. Move the meat to a plastic ziplock bag or covered container. Add 2 to 3 tablespoons of the citrus juices to the bag and marinate 1 to 8 hours in the refrigerator, turning occasionally. Set remaining citrus juices aside.

Remove the meat, reserving the marinade, and pat dry with a paper towel. Heat the drippings or oil over medium-high heat in a large Dutch oven. Add the meat and brown on one side. When mahogany brown, turn and brown on second side. Continue until all sides are browned. Remove the meat and set aside. Remove all but 1 tablespoon of the fat, if desired.

Add the stock, reserved marinade, and tomatoes to the pan, and bring to the boil; boil for 1 or 2 minutes. Taste and add a pinch of sugar if necessary. Reduce the heat to a simmer and add the meat back to the pot. Cover with foil then a lid, and cook covered until the meat is tender, 1 ½ to 2 hours on the stovetop or in a 350-degree oven.

Remove the roast and allow to cool. Remove any obvious fat from the top of the sauce. Bring to the boil and boil until thick, about 15 minutes. If possible, chill to remove all the fat when it comes to the top (preferably after sitting overnight).

Slice the cold meat and return it to the sauce. When ready to eat, add herbs, season to taste with remaining lime and lemon juice, salt, and pepper and reheat on the stovetop. Serve hot, topped with some or all of the remaining grated rind of limes and lemons. Any extra rind can be wrapped and refrigerated or frozen, separately.

N O T E : Mashed or smashed potatoes, white rice or wild rice, or noodles make cozy beds for stews and pot roasts.

# MUSSEL MEMORY

Tonight, as I scrub mussels for dinner, removing their beards, and carefully lifting them from the water so the sand is left in the sink, I remember the time when I became chef of C'an Poleta, a small country restaurant between Alcudia and Polensa, in Majorca, Spain. I had more courage than knowledge.

Having just received my Advanced Certificate from the London Cordon Bleu, I had never worked in a restaurant before and didn't really know what I didn't know. In fact, many years before, I had been convinced by my mother and friends that ladies didn't work in restaurants, and so I had given up the idea.

Then, one night, I asked the owner of a restaurant in Palma, where we were living for a few months, if I could hang around in the kitchen and observe for a few nights. She agreed, and, in the way that life has, the next day I was offered a job in the country, an hour from Palma, at what was reputed to be the best restaurant on the island. The French chef had quit because there were no women for him to date there, and the female New York owners were desperate enough to hire an inexperienced young woman as chef.

The deal was that all dinners were to be by reservation only so the kitchen could accommodate my pace, which was bound to be slower than the French chef's. But, as happens in so many restaurants, the desire for exclusivity, good food, and service was overcome by greed, and the maitre d' took all comers, reservations or no. Mussels were on the menu the first night.

When I was attending cooking school in England, I had scrubbed and cooked up many a batch of mussels for crowds of friends, so I felt confident. Of course, those mussels had come from the market. These mussels had come directly from the ocean, but I figured they were the same.

I hadn't reckoned on the Majorcan yellow jackets and hornets. I had assumed the windows of the kitchen were screened—after all, it's been hot there every summer for centuries. I was wrong. There were no screens anywhere. But there were venomous flying insects. And they liked me. They liked me a lot—seven bites in ten minutes' worth, just before we started serving.

With tears streaming down my cheeks from the bites, from frustration, from the fear of being the chef of a restaurant, I put the mussels on to cook. First I had put them in a big sink in the middle of the kitchen, covered them with ocean water, and scattered over them an oatmeal-type product to feed and plump them up before serving. The little Spanish maids who were my helpers had scrubbed them, removing their beards, and put them in the pan back in the sink in clean ocean water. I heated a pan and added the mussels. Still crying, I added salt and pepper. When their shiny black shells opened to show the sensuous flesh of the mussels inside, I sent them to the table where the proud owners sat, awaiting their first meal by their new chef.

Moments later, the two ladies who owned the restaurant stormed into the kitchen. It didn't take long to find out the source of their wrath! Unthinkingly, I had added salt to the water, then sent the mussels to the table without tasting their broth. The broth was so salty, the owners said, a spoon would have stood up in it. (I personally think they were exaggerating. Still, it was salty enough to be nearly inedible.) I began crying in earnest now. My first job in a kitchen, and I had blown it! Partly due to the flying creatures and partly because I had forgotten all the things I'd ever learned—most importantly, to taste, taste, taste.

The owners left the kitchen. After all, they couldn't fire me in the middle of the meal. And so we started a rocky relationship, which lasted until the season ended and our contract was up. They never did fire me, and I didn't quit. And I never again salted mussels until I was quite sure the broth needed flavoring! But I don't think they ever hired a novice cook again.

# SOUTHERN BOUILLABAISSE

Here's a fish muddle, or stew, to dream about. It has a long list of ingredients, but that makes it easier rather than harder.

It's written to elicit the best from the fish by adding the fish in a sequence to avoid overcooking. Cultivate your local seafood seller, for that is the best way to secure enough bones and fish scraps for a rich and flavorful broth. Since everything depends on a good broth, call a day or two ahead to reserve the fish and the bones. Hope for a fish head or two to enrich the broth. Lobster and shrimp shells are grand additions. If the bones or shells are frozen ahead of time they run a strong second to fresh but are better than none at all. The broth can be made ahead, strained, and frozen up to three months, or prepared that morning or the day ahead and refrigerated.

Making a marinade is something I learned from the *Grande Diplome Cooking Course,* edited by Anne Willan, and I am grateful for it. Although the croûtes are best when life is perfect and there is time to make them, store-bought are fine. The same thing is true of the sauce. Store-bought mayonnaise can be used to save time. The Pernod or anise ups the taste but doesn't cause the broth to have a licorice flavor. The amount can be adjusted according to the broth, or white wine can be added if there is no liqueur available.

SERVES 8 TO 10

**BROTH**

1–2 pounds of fish bones, heads, trimmings, etc.

Shrimp shells

1 fennel bulb, divided

2 heaping tablespoons fennel or anise seed

1–2 slices onion

1–2 garlic cloves

3 quarts water

**MARINADE & SOUP**

½–¾ cup olive oil, divided

8–10 garlic cloves, finely chopped (about ½ cup), divided

2 tablespoons saffron threads, divided

3 pounds assorted fresh South Atlantic fish (snapper, grouper, flounder, mahi mahi, sea trout, or sheepshead)

1 pound raw shrimp, in shell

2 blue crabs, optional

3 onions, chopped

2 leeks, chopped, optional

1 pound diced fresh tomatoes or 1 (14 ½-ounce)
   can tomatoes

Grated rind of 1 orange, no white attached

Salt

Freshly ground black pepper

1 pound littleneck clams, optional

1–2 tablespoons Pernod or anise liqueur

**CROÛTES & ROUILLE**

2 baguettes

3/4 cup olive oil, plus extra for croûtes

10 garlic cloves, chopped (½ cup)

½ teaspoon paprika

¼ teaspoon cayenne pepper

½ teaspoon salt

1 egg yolk

Make the broth. Discard any gills and innards of the fish, as well as any skin with scales. Rinse cavity of fish. Add fish bones and skin to a large pot, as well as any shrimp shells. Remove the exterior layer of the fennel—the stalky portions coming out from the bulb—and some of the fronds. Chop the bulb and fronds and reserve, separately, for later use. Add the fennel stalks, fennel or anise seed, sliced onion, and garlic cloves and enough water to cover all the bones. Bring to the boil; reduce heat to low, cover, and simmer 20 to 25 minutes. Set aside uncovered until needed. Strain, pushing the bones enough to be sure that all the broth is used. Discard the bones. Taste the broth and adjust seasonings. It should measure 2 or 3 quarts. If less, add water. If more, bring to the boil and boil down to 3 quarts.

Meanwhile, make the marinade for the fish by mixing 6 tablespoons of olive oil and 2 tablespoons chopped garlic. Soak 1 tablespoon of the saffron threads in a couple of tablespoons hot water and add to the olive oil and garlic mixture.

Cut the 3 pounds skinned and boned fish into 2-inch cubes, keeping separate according to type and thickness. Sort out any small scraps and set aside to add last. Toss the fish in the saffron marinade and refrigerate in a plastic bag until needed. Clean the shrimp and crabs.

Heat ⅓ cup of oil over medium heat in a very large pot. Add the onions, leeks, and reserved chopped fennel bulb to the hot oil and sauté until soft, about 10 minutes, taking care not to brown. Add 5 table-spoons garlic and sauté 1 minute more. Add the tomatoes, a bunch of the reserved fennel fronds, and the orange rind. Bring the soup to the boil, reduce heat to low, and cook 10 minutes. Add the remaining saffron to a couple tablespoons of the strained broth. Add remaining broth and saffron mixture to the tomato sauce and increase heat to medium high. Bring soup to the boil, reduce heat to low, and simmer 30 to 40 minutes, until extremely flavorful. Season to taste with salt and pepper, remembering that seafood is still to be added.

> CONTINUED

Meanwhile, make the croûtes. Cut one of the baguettes into ½-inch slices, brush with olive oil and bake in 350- degree oven until golden brown. Cut the remaining baguette into large pieces and place in a food processor or blender to make breadcrumbs. Remove all but ⅓ cup of the breadcrumbs, saving any extra for another use. Add roughly three-fourths of the garlic to the breadcrumbs in the food processor and process until finely chopped. Add ½ cup of the soup broth, paprika, cayenne, salt, and egg yolk. Purée until smooth. Add the oil slowly, as you would in a mayonnaise or aïoli, and process again until smooth. Taste the mixture, add the rest of the garlic as needed, and adjust seasonings. Refrigerate covered until needed.

When ready to eat, return the soup to the boil. (If it will not cover the seafood, add enough water to cover.) Reduce the heat slightly, add the fish incrementally according to thickness, starting with the thickest pieces of fish, and cook a few minutes without letting it boil hard. Add the shrimp, crabs, and the thinner or more delicate fish, such as flounder, and cook 1 or 2 minutes in the simmering soup. Add the optional littleneck clams and any remaining scraps of fish. Cook until the shrimp and crabs are pink and the clams open. Remove all the seafood and put on a hot platter.

Season the soup with salt and pepper and Pernod or anise liqueur. Boil down quickly if necessary to increase flavor. Sprinkle fish with chopped fennel frond if desired. Serve the soup and platter of fish separately, or mix and serve together. Top croûtes with rouille and serve with soup.

# First Fish

It was a cold and choppy day when we set out from shore to go fishing, and if I hadn't said I'd go, I would have stayed at home. But I was committed and making the best of it. I had dressed for the occasion with a sweatshirt and blue jeans over my bathing suit, socks up to my knees, and tennis shoes, not rubber sandals. But I wished I had galoshes.

Suddenly, after an hour of misery, the weather lifted and the motor stopped smelling so vile, and the boat stopped rocking. The sun greeted us as an old friend, tanning us with warmth and radiance above the reflected sea. With the sea and sun as our only comrades, my friend and I lolled under the clear sky, laughing and talking and reading short stories and making up limericks, giggling at the globs of protective cream on our noses and tummies. And we caught a few fish.

Most of them were small bluefish. The larger ones we either didn't know how to catch or they weren't coming in that close to shore. I landed my first fish at the end of the day. We packed all the fish in ice, and a willing fisherman cleaned them for a small consideration on the tiny dock. It was my time to cook, and we were eager.

When the sea and sun marry with laughter, there's avhungry completeness that seasons the food. Coupled with the smell of sea on clothes and hair, and the pride of achievement, anticipation dances on a high wire before the meal.

I broiled my bluefish in a flat enamel plate/lid, with a little wine and butter. I was proud of my fish, my first fish, and arrogantly carried him to the table. Somehow, I slid and stumbled and my fish gently slithered out onto the floor. I nearly wept. My friend, dear soul, knew my anguish, and slipped a spatula under my fish and placed him back on the platter, saying, "We won't eat the skin on the bottom where he touched the floor." My tears dried on their way to my cheek, and we looked out the window at our friend the sun traveling down the sky and talked and marveled at the specialness of simple fresh fish.

# WHOLE ROASTED SNAPPER

When buying a whole fish, the first thing to look for is bright, clear eyes. Next comes a clean, light odor. Snappers can be any number of fish, with thick skin and scales as large as tiddlywinks to lightly red skin and delicate, mild flesh. If in doubt, question the seller as to age and type. I like to cook fish with the head on, but if you don't, try to save the head for fish stock. You are paying for it whether you use it or not. If snapper is not available, any light, white-fleshed fish will do. Either Aïoli (page 104) or Virginia Willis's Peanut Romesco Sauce (page 105) would be a flavorful addition added atop or alongside each serving.

SERVES 2 TO 4

1 (2-pound) whole snapper or other whole white fish, head on, cleaned and scaled

4 tablespoons melted butter or oil, cook's preference

Salt

Freshly ground black pepper

1/4 cup fresh lemon juice, optional

Virginia Willis's Peanut Romesco Sauce (page 105), Aïoli Sauce (page 104), optional

Preheat oven to 450 degrees. Line a rimmed baking sheet with heavy aluminum foil and oil it, or oil an oven-to-table baking dish. Rinse and pat the fish dry with paper towels, taking care to ensure the cavity is clean.

Make 2 to 4 diagonal slashes in the skin of the fish (top side only). Move to the prepared pan or dish and brush both sides with butter or oil. Season to taste with salt and pepper. Pour on the lemon juice, if using.

Measure the thickness of the fish from the foil to the top side of the fish at its thickest part. Roast uncovered for 9 minutes to the inch of thickness, until meat is firm to the touch and springs back. The fish is done when its thickest part registers approximately 135 degrees on an instant-read thermometer.

Slide the fish off the foil using two large spatulas or any number of fish gadgets. Peel off the skin with a knife. The top will be prettier than the bottom, so serve any guests first. Use two large implements to slide the flesh off the bone and onto the plate. When the top flesh is removed, flip over the body of the

> CONTINUED

fish and serve the bottom flesh, using the same method, avoiding any bones. The cheek is regarded as particularly desirable, as it is tender and flavorful, so serve it to the most revered guest. Serve with Romesco or Aïoli, if desired.

**VARIATIONS:**

- Stuff the cavity with lemon slices and herbs.

- Stuff the cavity with stalks of lemongrass and broken makrut lime leaves (discard before serving).

# AÏOLI

This sauce is one I first started making in Majorca when I was chef at a restaurant. I'd never tasted aïoli before then and didn't know that other Mediterranean countries have a variation—allioli, different in spelling and pronunciation as well as ingredients. Aïoli also varies considerably with the type of oil used, so make sure the oil is one that will go well in the final product. Slaw, for instance, would be better with a neutral oil such as canola or other vegetable oil rather than olive oil—unless adding chopped peanuts, when peanut oil would suit better. Sometimes I mix oils, like olive oil and peanut oil.

For allioli, extra virgin olive oil is the standard. It can be used as a separate dipping sauce, as with snails, shrimp, and other small foods, or can be used as a sauce with a beef tenderloin or snapper, or even as a rouille stirred into a fish soup or bouillabaisse when a lot of cayenne pepper is used.

MAKES 1 ½ CUPS

4 cloves garlic

3 egg yolks

3 tablespoons fresh lemon juice, divided

¼–½ teaspoon Dijon mustard

Salt

1 tablespoon water

1 ½ cups oil, cook's preference

Freshly ground black pepper

Cayenne pepper, to taste

Add garlic to the bowl of a food processor fitted with the metal blade. Chop finely then remove and set aside. Add egg yolks, lemon juice, mustard, salt, and 1 tablespoon water to the food processor (no need to clean it in between). Process until the egg yolks are thick and lemon-colored. (Or crush garlic in a mortar and pestle, then proceed with recipe using a whisk and a mixing bowl.)

With the food processor running, gradually add in one-third of the oil, drop by drop at first, until the mixture becomes cohesive. Continue processing, adding the remaining oil in a slow, steady stream, until mixture is thick and the oil is incorporated.

Season to taste with the remaining lemon juice, salt, black pepper, and cayenne. If a lighter mayonnaise is needed, add 1 or 2 more tablespoons water. Keep covered and refrigerated no longer than a week.

## VIRGINIA WILLIS'S PEANUT ROMESCO SAUCE

Virginia Willis is one of my beloved students who has surpassed me. I think her use of roasted peanuts is very clever and tasty, although the traditional nut for this recipe is almonds. This recipe is adapted from her book *Secrets of the Southern Table*.

MAKES ABOUT 3 CUPS

½ cup roasted peanuts or almonds

1 (12-ounce) jar roasted red bell peppers, drained

½ cup tomato purée

3 garlic cloves, divided

1 slice country white bread, toasted and crumbled

1 tablespoon smoked paprika

⅓ cup sherry vinegar

⅔–1 cup extra virgin olive oil, divided

Coarse kosher salt

Freshly ground black pepper

Grind the peanuts or almonds in a food processor. Add the roasted peppers, tomato purée, 2 of the garlic cloves, bread, and paprika. Process to a paste. Add the vinegar and pulse to blend. With the food processor running, gradually pour ⅔ cup of oil through the feed tube in a steady stream until the mixture thickens like mayonnaise. Taste and adjust for seasoning with salt and pepper, adding garlic and olive oil as needed. Transfer to a serving bowl if serving immediately, or store covered in the refrigerator.

# Way to a Man's Heart

She never saw a harvest moon without thinking of him and the duck that flew for them the night of a full moon. From shrimp to duck, the story of a love affair.

When he first told her he loved her, it was while eating shrimp from the Georgia coast. "You're wonderful," he said. The way to a man's heart is his stomach.

He said he loved her food. She woke up planning what she wanted to feed him for dinner. She became more desperately in love as time went on, even as the relationship began to deteriorate. He was frequently late for dinner and too busy to call. Her grocery menus were frantically made, obsessive lists of things she wanted to cook for him—asparagus, roast duck, chocolate mousse. The way to a man's heart is his stomach.

One night they made plans for dinner out. She would rather have cooked for him—to have exercised her culinary prowess. He wanted control, to be free of her food, and made reservations at a country restaurant an hour's drive away. She decided she had to have her hair done for him so he would tell her again she was beautiful. Her hairdresser was running late and she sat in the beauty shop, trapped and full of foreboding. She arrived home and he was sitting on the doorstep, silently, angrily waiting, his control thwarted.

There was a full harvest moon, their dominant companion as they drove, with the smell of her harshly permanented, now frizzy and ugly hair filling the car. They squabbled about her being late, at the distance he was choosing to drive rather than eat her cooking. He didn't say she was beautiful. She had to force herself to breathe through the pain in her chest.

They arrived at the allegedly romantic restaurant only to find it nearly closed, wearily patient waiters holding the dinners he had preordered. They sat alone in the empty dining room. When she cut into her duck, it was so tough it flew off the plate and slid down his starched white shirt front. Distressed, she still couldn't suppress a grin. He said she had done it on purpose. She hadn't, but might have if she'd thought of it. He stormed out and waited in the car. Picking the duck off the floor, she told the stunned waiter to bring the check. Her rage at her love's rejection of all she was rippled through her physically. They had a violent fight in the light of the moon. When her hysterics abated, they drove the long way home in silence, and separated for a long time.

Ten years later, after he had married and divorced another and they were together again, she wanted him to eat a duck she had cooked herself. She took it on a trip to the mountains. They remembered that night with uneasy laughter, recalling what they might have lost. She had cooked many ducks since then with crisp-tender skins. And she always removed the backbone and ribs. One had never shot off her plate again. After all, the way to a man's heart is his stomach.

# DIXIE CASSOULET

Cassoulet, most likely the basis for the word "casserole," is traditionally baked in an earthenware pot and served with a gratin of breadcrumbs on the top. I use a sturdy enamel pot to make sure it doesn't cook too rapidly. Cozy and comforting, this bean dish (field peas are part of the bean family) is always welcome for a winter party, where a cassoulet goes a long way served alongside a green salad. It takes little of the cook's time, cooking happily by itself unattended for hours. I make it over the course of a few days, but it can be done in one day. Use a good stock. If you like, ignore some of the ingredients and their amounts, as nothing is essential. Dixie Cassoulet is easily made ahead and reheated, or frozen and reheated.

SERVES 25

2 pounds dry field peas, white acre peas, lady peas, or other small peas, or 4 to 6 pounds fresh or frozen

4 cups duck, goose, pork, or other flavorful fat

6 large onions, chopped

8 garlic cloves, finely chopped

1 fennel bulb

2 quarts strong chicken, turkey, duck, or goose stock, preferably homemade

Salt

Freshly ground black pepper

1 cup finely chopped fresh parsley, divided

½ cup chopped fresh thyme, divided

3 tablespoons tomato paste

3 cups white wine or chicken stock

24 sweet Italian-style sausage links, pork or turkey (about 6 pounds)

2 tablespoon coriander seeds

2 tablespoon fennel seeds

1–2 teaspoons cumin seeds

6 cups fresh breadcrumbs or panko

Prepare the beans. Defrost if frozen. Soak dried beans in water to cover overnight, or cover with water in a pan, bring to the boil, cover, and set aside for 1 hour. Drain the water before proceeding. Melt enough of the fat over medium heat in a large, heavy frying pan to cover the bottom of the pan. Add the chopped onions and cook until soft. Add garlic and cook 2 minutes more. Remove the exterior layer of the fennel—the stalky portions coming out from the bulb—and some of the fronds and set aside for another purpose. Chop the fennel bulb, add to the onions, and cook 5 or so minutes.

Add half the cooked onion, fennel, and garlic mixture and the beans to a heavy 6-quart pot, and reserve the rest in the frying pan. Cover the bean mixture with some of the stock; cover with a lid and

> CONTINUED

cook over medium heat, stirring occasionally, until the beans are soft, about 1 ½ to 2 hours. Check and add stock to cover as needed. When soft, taste and season well with salt and pepper. Stir in half the parsley and half the thyme.

Add the tomato paste along with the wine (or stock) to the onion-garlic mixture still in the frying pan. Bring to the boil, and boil until reduced by half, just a few minutes.

Prick the sausage on all sides. Heat a little of the duck fat over medium heat in a large frying pan. Working in batches, add sausages and sauté until brown on all sides, adding more fat as needed. Cut into bite-sized pieces and add to the tomato mixture along with half of the remaining parsley and thyme. Crush the coriander, fennel, and cumin seeds using a mortar and pestle or rolling pin. Season the tomato mixture with a portion of the crushed seeds, tasting as necessary. Add salt and freshly ground pepper to taste.

Add a portion of the crushed seeds to the beans, along with salt and pepper to taste. Layer the beans and the tomato/sausage mixture in a large 10 to 12-quart pot, starting with a third of the beans then half of the tomato/sausage mixture. Repeat, finishing with the last third of the beans. Add stock to barely cover the beans. Bring to the boil on top of the stove, stir thoroughly and remove from heat.

Mix the breadcrumbs with remaining parsley and thyme. Layer the top of the cassoulet with a portion of the breadcrumbs. Dot generously with duck fat.

Move the pot to a rimmed baking sheet and bake in the middle of a 350-degree oven until the crumb gratin is golden brown (about 30 minutes). Push the gratin down into the beans with a large spoon. Cover again with a layer of the breadcrumb mixture. Dot with more fat. Return to oven. Repeat as often as desired, completing up to 8 gratins but no fewer than 2. Each gratin takes 30 to 60 minutes to be ready to be pushed into the beans. Be sure to taste after each gratin layer, adding any seasoning and liquid as desired. When ready, either leave in the oven to serve warm, or remove from the oven, let cool to moderate, and store covered in the refrigerator for 1 or 2 days, or freeze, until ready to use. Several hours before serving, move the cassoulet to the countertop and let come to room temperature. Move to a baking sheet and reheat 1 hour or so. The cassoulet may be frozen when cool enough, and even reheated when frozen, which will obviously take a much longer time.

**VARIATION:** If a duck or goose was roasted for its fat, add its meat to the cassoulet.

# PAT CONROY'S
# SPINACH TORTELLINI SALAD

Pat Conroy, the South Carolina author, loved cooking and was once a student of mine, long before he moved to Italy. This was the pasta he made, and we served it to all sorts of famous people in his apartment rooftop garden in Rome, Italy, at Cynthia and Cliff's wedding supper, on the hottest night of many years.

SERVES 12

1 pound spinach tortellini stuffed with Parmesan cheese, preferably fresh

½ cup red wine vinegar

1 teaspoon Dijon mustard

1 cup extra virgin olive oil

Salt

Freshly ground black pepper

1 teaspoon granulated sugar, optional

1 ½ cups grated imported Parmesan cheese

1 cup pitted green olives, chopped

½ pound cooked ham, sliced in small finger-sized strips

4 tablespoons chopped fresh basil or thyme, optional

Bring large pot of generously salted water to the boil over high heat. Cook pasta until al dente, then drain.

Meanwhile, mix vinegar and mustard in a bowl. Slowly whisk in the oil. Taste for seasoning and add salt, and pepper. Correct vinegar with sugar, if needed. If kept in an airtight container, vinaigrette will stay fresh almost indefinitely in the refrigerator or in a cool room.

Toss warm pasta with Parmesan, olives, and ham then dress with vinaigrette as needed. Add salt, pepper, and optional herbs and serve warm. Can be made ahead and chilled, but bring to room temperature before serving, or reheat in microwave.

# Roman Banquet

One hot, sultry July morning I woke up yearning for a melon like the ones I found for the wedding supper I had fixed July 7 in Rome, Italy, when friends decided to marry there. A perfect melon is sweet, cool, thirst-quenching, juicy, a foil for Italy's beloved Parma ham, prosciutto. In fact, I craved not just the melon but the result of the marriage of opposites: a ripe, tender wedge of melon wrapped with the slightly salty, richly flavorful aged prosciutto, which cloaks the melon like a sheer, flesh-colored gown.

The Italian melon looks like a small cantaloupe, a bit larger than a softball, and its perfume announces its presence even before you cut it. I have never had a melon like it in the States.

I prepared this prenuptial wedding feast for beautiful Cynthia Stevens, the talented producer of my television show, who married Atlanta's long-time bachelor Cliff Graubart. Lenore Conroy, with help from her husband, Pat, had done most of the shopping for the thirty-five people we were expecting for dinner at their home in Rome. But there was still shopping to be done, so we walked, plastic bags in hand, across the Tiber to an outdoor market. There we bought branches of fresh rosemary, bunches of basil and marjoram, Lenore sniffing, critiquing, and holding out for the very best. We searched the stalls for two more melons, holding them to our noses to be sure they were fragrant.

At another stall, the man who sold us the cherries exclaimed, "They are better than a night of love." Seeing our reddened faces, he quickly declared he was not flirting, just telling us how good they were. Tasting one, we thought they were good, although perhaps not "that" good, but good enough to send Cliff and Cynthia on their way.

At the poultry shop we picked up the chickens, Cornish hens, and quail, all split up the backbone for us. The poultry man asked if the hens were for a very traditional Italian dish for these birds called "diablo." "No," we exclaimed, horrified, "for a wedding." Fresh bread completed our task, and we trudged home loaded with sacks, stopping to re-shift our bundles on the narrow streets full of old-world charm.

When we returned, Pat was proudly boiling water for the stuffed spinach tortellini for his cold pasta salad and had already removed the pits from a mound of tiny green Italian olives. The coupling of the olives and the tortellini was aided by a salad dressing of oil and vinegar and fresh herbs in abundance as well as heaping quantities of freshly grated Parmigiano-Reggiano and slices of ham.

The poultry was marinated in lemon juice, which had been squeezed by the Conroys' young daughter, then drizzled with olive oil before being roasted in the tiny oven. The birds were lovely, their skin brown and crisp and their flesh moist. All were piled in a beautiful stack and sprinkled with herbs and the reduced juices. (The oven blew its fuse twice, and we had to stop and do other things.)

We sliced heart-red tomatoes and splashed them with rich olive oil. We peeled the roasted sweet red peppers and tore them into strips to be mated with aged balsamic vinegar.

As we worked, we listened to calls through the open window from the convent next door that had been turned into a prison for men. "I want a lawyer," wailed one man, followed by a different echo, "I want a woman." All the time a guard paced the catwalk with his Uzi machine gun, and the birds—swallows—circled overhead with a taunt of freedom.

The inmates were blessedly silent by the time we were ready for dinner, and the sun was blushing good night as we toasted Cynthia and Cliff. Pat Conroy orated a history of their life and love, and the story was so tender it brought us to tears. We finished the evening sucking the cherries from their pits and thinking the melons, not the cherries, were really better than a night of love.

# LEMON FETTUCCINE

One of my great pleasures has been to make pasta with some of our grandchildren when they were young. I use my pasta machine very little now but keep it on hand just in case. Now fresh pasta is readily available. If it's not available, of course boxed fettuccine is fine to use.

SERVES 4

1 lemon

1 ½ cups dry white wine

¾ cup heavy cream, to taste

1 pound fettuccine, preferably fresh

3 tablespoons butter, in pieces

1 cup freshly grated Parmesan cheese

1 to 2 tablespoons extra virgin olive oil, optional

Salt

Freshly ground black pepper

Using a knife or vegetable peeler, remove rind from the lemon, avoiding any white pith. Slice the peel into thin matchsticks. Juice the lemon, strain and reserve. Place matchsticks in a large nonreactive pan with the wine and bring to the boil over high heat. Reduce heat to medium high and cook until it reduces to a syrupy mixture, about ¼ cup, about 10 minutes.

Remove from heat, pour in about ¼ cup of the cream, and stir. Then pour in remaining cream and stir as needed. Return to stove and bring to the boil over high heat. Reduce heat and simmer until it is thickened and reduced slightly, about 5 minutes. Remove from heat and set aside. This is your cream sauce.

Meanwhile, bring large pot of generously salted water to boil. Cook pasta until al dente, save a bit of the pasta water, then drain.

Return hot pasta pot to stove. Pour in the cream sauce, butter and lemon juice, stir, then return hot drained pasta to the pan and add a few tablespoons of cooking water. Toss together and add cheese in three or four parts, tossing each to meld with sauce. Add more cooking water if sauce is too thick and crumbly. Ladle onto plates and drizzle each portion with olive oil, if using. Season to taste with salt and pepper.

# SIDE
# DISHES

Restaurants have made the concept of side dishes quite different from what I grew up with. Then, side dishes were actually served on the side, not under the main course meat. At the dinner table sides were in separate bowls, or on children's plates beside the main course meat, but of course, not touching if the child didn't want them to.

Seeing sides intertwined with the main courses on restaurant menus as well as on plates and thereby touching, seems a bit odd to me. Even odder is the fact that a side may make a crispy main course soggy.

So, here we have everything from salads to zucchini as sides; you can add your main course on top if it pleases you.

# SALAD OF BABY GREENS

While modern greens are available prewashed and packaged, it is important to know how to wash them. Fill a bowl with cold water and add the greens. Swish the greens in the cold water then remove the greens to a colander. Discard the water once the greens have been removed. If necessary to remove more debris, repeat the process. Traditionally, greens are to be washed three times, but they seem less dirty from our local farms these days.

In making a green salad, use one or a combination of the following: baby turnip or spinach greens; arugula or watercress; red leaf, Bibb, Boston, or other tender lettuces; and as many whole herbs as are tasty on their own. Chop whatever herbs need chopping and add them.

SERVES 6 TO 8

5 cups baby greens

1–2 tablespoons whole or chopped fresh basil, thyme, oregano, tarragon, lemon balm, and/or mint

⅓–½ cup Basic Vinaigrette (page 121)

Toss the cleaned and dried greens with the chopped herbs and vinaigrette just before serving.

.

## DRESSING A SALAD

Dress a green salad just before serving to prevent the leaves from wilting and browning from acid in the vinaigrette. Add the greens to a large, wide bowl. Drizzle dressing on top. Toss with clean hands or salad implements to coat the leaves lightly in dressing. Add more dressing as needed. If serving from the larger bowl and passing at the table, pass as soon as possible.

# BASIC VINAIGRETTE

Salad dressings, like vinaigrettes, are an integral part of the home kitchen. Rather than a line up of partly used bottles of commercial dressings, try using homemade where you know the ingredients and can control fats and sugar among other additions. I normally use a light olive oil for mine but have used peanut and canola. I do avoid many other oils, as they tend to go "off" with the heat of the Southern kitchen more than others in my experience. The better the ingredients, the better the dressing. Taste each of them separately as well as once combined. Too oily? Add salt, a bit of sugar, or a lighter oil to lighten it. Too tart? Add water or stock before adding more oil to balance.

Don't be afraid to experiment with adding citrus juices, sweeteners, herbs, spices, or anything that changes the texture.

SERVES 4 TO 6

1–2 teaspoons Dijon mustard

⅓ cup sherry vinegar (or substitute red wine, Champagne, or other wine vinegar)

1 teaspoon water

Salt

Freshly ground black pepper

1 cup extra virgin olive oil

Granulated sugar, optional

Water or chicken stock or broth

For an everyday vinaigrette, whisk or shake together mustard, vinegar, water, salt, pepper, and oil. Taste and add more seasoning, sugar, and/or water or chicken stock. Refrigerate up to a week; whisk or shake as needed.

For a temporary emulsion, whisk the mustard, vinegar, water, salt, and pepper together in a small bowl. Slowly whisk in a fourth of the oil until thick. Add the rest in a steady stream while whisking. Season to taste with additional salt. Add sugar and/or water or chicken stock if still too oily-tasting. This vinaigrette will be opaque and creamy, with the ingredients evenly distributed. Store covered in the refrigerator or on the counter.

**VARIATIONS:** For a small portion of vinaigrette, whisk together 1 teaspoon mustard, 1 tablespoon vinegar, salt, pepper, and 3 tablespoons oil. Taste for seasoning and add sugar or water or chicken stock if desired.

• Use heavy cream rather than oil for a creamy vinaigrette.

• Add 1 chopped garlic clove; a chopped shallot or green onion; a favorite chopped herb (such as thyme, oregano, or basil); a bit of curry powder, ground coriander, or cumin; or substitute honey for the sugar.

# WATERMELON AND CANTALOUPE SALAD

There is a wonderful restaurant in the south of France that specializes in the lovely French Charentais melon—my favorite of any melon I have eaten—where I once took a cooking class with my son-in-law Pierre Henri's mother, following which I ate more melon recipes than I considered possible. I lie in bed and dream of them at night, as well as the ripe watermelon and cantaloupes Cynthia and I gathered on a photo shoot in Cordele, Georgia, one summer day and stored in the wings of the Georgia Secretary of Agriculture's plane. Secretary Irwin had kindly loaned us his plane to fly to agricultural places that were difficult to reach. Since most picking in South Georgia is done in the cool of morning (if there is any cool), so was our melon-picking. We picked the ones with the widest expanse of white where the melon had sat, ripening everywhere but its belly. The paler green belly, evenly webbed rind, and the "give" of the stems award big kudos to cantaloupes, honeydews, and watermelons.

There is nothing better than ripe melon from the field. We rarely encounter it in our urban life, so we bring home and ripen our own melons as we do many of our avocados, tomatoes, and other fruits, on the top of our kitchen table. The aroma of the melons is by far the headiest of the fruits. When ready to eat, we start with a salad, beginning with equal amounts of each melon cut in bite-sized cubes of 1 or 2 inches, adding as we go along. The ripe melons in themselves provide enough juices, but there is always the option of a sauce or even a splash of white wine or wine vinegar for the salad. One kind of melon is better than none, two kinds make a good splash of color and flavor for any table, and three are heaven.

Other additions can be arugula, lemon balm, mint, lemon or orange thyme, ripe bite-sized tomatoes, halved grapes, or the cook's delight. Usually the melon speaks for itself. Although we are constantly told that melons don't ripen once picked, I still think melons that have softened on the counter have more flavor than harder ones, so I don't refrigerate until soft.

3 cups melon, preferably two varieties, cut in ½- to 1-inch cubes

Splash of white wine, or white wine vinegar, optional

1–2 tablespoons chopped fresh herbs (see headnote), optional

2 cups arugula or sturdy lettuce, optional

Tomatoes, grapes, etc., optional

Combine all ingredients in a bowl, toss gently, refrigerate 1 to 2 days as desired. Serve cold.

**NOTE:** Any leftover melon can be puréed to use in Melon Soup (page 46).

# CAROLINA GOLD RICE & FRUIT SALAD WITH GINGER DRESSING

This can be served—and extolled—just as it is, or cooked meat such as ham, chicken, or fish can be added for a more elaborate dish. It can even be served hot or cold.

SERVES 6

½ cup Carolina Gold Rice,* Arborio, or other short-grained rice

½ cup pecan pieces

1 teaspoon curry powder

1 cup fresh or dried figs, quartered

½ cup dried apricots, quartered

1 recipe Ginger Dressing (page 125)

3–4 cups arugula or other tasty greens, washed and dried

Bring a large pot of salted water to the boil. Add rice, reduce to simmer, and cook until the center of a grain has only a small amount of white when cut with a fingernail, about 15 minutes. Stir occasionally to prevent it from sticking to the bottom of the pot. Drain and rinse under cold water.

Toast the pecans over medium-low heat in a small skillet until golden brown. Remove to a bowl. Add curry powder to the empty skillet and toast gently just until fragrant, about 30 to 60 seconds. Add to the bowl with pecans.

In a large bowl, toss the figs, apricots, pecan-curry mixture, and cooled rice with about ¼ cup of the Ginger Dressing until lightly coated; add the arugula. Taste and add more seasoning or dressing if needed.

**VARIATION:** Substitute a favorite grain such as Basmati brown rice, red rice, pearl barley, rye berries, wheat berries, farro, or the like.

*Carolina Gold may need rinsing.

# GINGER DRESSING

I'm such a ginger fan that a friend once gave me a pound of candied ginger. I use it with savory recipes as well as sweet, as I rarely see what's "not to like" about ginger. Without boiled ginger juice, grated ginger and white wine vinegar would be a likely substitute but might take a little adjustment.

MAKES ½ CUP

1 tablespoon bottled ginger juice

2 tablespoons white wine or sherry vinegar

Salt

⅓ cup extra virgin olive oil

Whisk the ginger juice, vinegar, optional hot sauce, and a couple of big pinches of salt in a large bowl. Whisk in the olive oil, but stop when the dressing takes on a slightly thick, opaque look. Use to dress the salad just before serving, or store for up to one week in the refrigerator.

# ASPARAGUS SALAD

Asparagus was once a major crop in South Carolina, shipped straight up to New York and other northern cities. Somehow canned asparagus took over in my childhood and I hated it and its texture. Fresh asparagus is not only in my good graces, I love it.

SERVES 2

6–10 asparagus stalks, preferably thin

¼–½ cup grated Parmigiano-Reggiano cheese

¼–⅓ cup extra virgin olive oil

1–2 teaspoons sherry vinegar or lemon juice

Salt and pepper

Cut off any rough ends of the asparagus stalks. Peel asparagus, starting at the bottom of the flower. If the stalk is slender and young, save the peel. If tough, use for another purpose. Continue peeling the stalk, essentially making ribbons of asparagus. Gather them and any delicate outer peels into a small mound and toss with Parmigiano-Reggiano and olive oil. Add sherry vinegar or lemon juice. Season with salt and pepper to taste.

# ALMA'S NEW POTATOES WITH MUSTARD SEED

Alma Friedman and I worked at Rich's Department Store at the same time, where she ruled the Advertising Department with a firm hand, and I was Director of the Cooking School. Not a cook herself, when she tasted something she liked she would ask me to duplicate it. Usually her choice was so good that the dish stayed in my repertoire. I still use this recipe about twice a month but usually cut it in half or just guesstimate for Jack and myself. After all, I didn't have a recipe to begin with, so I might come up with a new one. So might you, for that matter. Feel free to embellish.

### SERVES 10

40–50 new potatoes, about 3–4 pounds

½ cup bacon or meat drippings or butter

5–6 tablespoons mustard seed

5–6 tablespoons Dijon mustard, to taste

Salt

Freshly ground black pepper

Preheat the oven to 350 degrees.

Peel the potatoes. Heat the drippings or butter in a roasting pan over medium heat, add the potatoes, and toss to coat with the drippings. Place in the oven and roast, turning every 15 minutes, until browned all over, about 1 hour. Remove from the oven, toss in the mustard seed, and return to the oven for another 5 minutes. Remove and add the Dijon mustard, tossing with a spoon to coat the potatoes lightly. Add salt and pepper to taste. Serve hot and savor.

# ANNA'S POTATO CAKE

This derivation of the French Pommes Anna is served upside down, revealing a brown, crispy, buttery exterior and a tender, moist interior. It is a special dish but an easy one if using a heavy, nonstick skillet. It is doable otherwise but a bit more stressful. Of course, it may be prepared in a smaller or larger amount and pan, depending on the number of people being served. I've tried adding cheese or other ingredients, but I like the original way noted here for the contrast of crisp and soft and the heightened taste of the potatoes. Remember, water follows salt, so salting too early in the process will dilute the crustiness and its color. Neglecting to add salt every other layer will prevent the potatoes from sticking together.

SERVES 4 TO 6

1 ½–1 ¾ pounds Yukon Gold potatoes, peeled
   and sliced ⅛ inch thick*

Salt

Freshly ground black pepper

5–8 tablespoons butter, cut in pieces

Preheat oven to 400 degrees.

Thickly butter a 6- to 8-inch heavy, nonstick, well-seasoned frying pan, or cake tin. Arrange the potatoes in overlapping circles to cover the base of the pan, making a pretty design as it will be the final top crust. Add a second layer, continuing to overlap, and season with salt and pepper; dot with 4 to 5 pieces of butter. Continue to fill the pan with layers of potatoes (the first two layers and the last layer are the only ones that need to be pretty—the rest can be haphazard), seasoning and buttering every other layer. Butter a piece of aluminum foil and cover the potatoes and the pan. Put an ovenproof plate or a heavy saucepan on top of the foil to press down on the potatoes.

Cook the potatoes in the pan on the stovetop over medium heat for 10 to 15 minutes to brown the bottom, checking to be sure it is not burning. When medium brown—the color of light caramel—move the pan to the oven, leaving the weighted ovenproof plate on, if possible. Bake about 30 minutes, or until the potatoes are soft, depending on the number of potatoes. Can be made ahead to this point and set aside if necessary, then reheated for 10 minutes, but it will suffer a bit. Using oven mitts, turn out upside down on a serving dish, crust side up. To serve, cut with a knife or scissors.

*Thicker slices will work, but the melting quality of the interior layers of the cake will decline a bit. A food processor or mandolin are handy slicing tools for the nonprofessional cook.

# WHIPPED, MASHED, OR RICED POTATOES

Once mastered, mashed potatoes can be cooked more frequently and served easily for a weeknight family meal. Some families like lumpy potatoes, as they are used to them. Others like them smooth, rich, and loose. It doesn't matter. But when a special meal comes around, consider the variation below and use cream. Mashed potatoes should be so delicious that the family will miss them long after the cook is dead and gone. And don't forget the butter. The recipe can be doubled if necessary.

SERVES 4

2 pounds Yukon Gold or Idaho potatoes, peeled and cut into ½-inch cubes

Salt

2–4 tablespoons butter, divided

½–1 cup milk, buttermilk, skim milk, or potato water, heated

Freshly ground black pepper

Add enough cold water to the potatoes to cover them by 1 inch in a heavy pot. Add 1 teaspoon salt and bring to the boil over high heat. Reduce the heat to low, cover, and simmer until soft, about 20 to 30 minutes. Test by squooshing a bit of potatoes between two fingers to make sure there are no lumps. If there are, cook longer. Drain well in a colander, reserving water as needed to add to mashed potatoes.

Add the butter to the empty pot and melt over low heat. Return potatoes to the pot over a low heat and whip, mash, or rice (see "Perfect Mashed Potatoes," page 133) to incorporate the butter. If the potatoes are more watery than desired, before adding the hot liquid, cook the potatoes with the butter until some of the liquid evaporates. Add some of the hot liquid and butter and blend well. Continue adding milk, mashing or whipping constantly, until the desired consistency is reached. Season to taste with salt and pepper.

> CONTINUED

**REHEATING MASHED POTATOES:** When cooking the potatoes a day or two in advance, cool and store in a heavy-duty ziplock bag. When ready to use, move mashed potatoes to a bowl, cover with plastic wrap to keep a skin from forming, and reheat in the microwave until very hot. Or heat a heavy pan with some butter over medium heat, add the potatoes, and stir over heat continually until hot.

## PERFECT MASHED POTATOES

There are three crucial steps in achieving this ideal: 1) cooking the potatoes sufficiently, 2) adding fat to the hot potatoes to coat the starch molecules, and 3) adding hot liquid to the potatoes in a pot over the heat to let the starches swell. To finish the potatoes, select one of these methods:

- Mash or whip in the fat over low heat, then add the hot liquid using a small electric hand mixer or sturdy whisk.

- Use a flat-bottomed masher or other heavy object to mash down the drained potatoes in the pan over low heat before stirring in hot liquid, and continue until desired texture.

- Push the cooked potatoes through a ricer into the still hot pan with melted butter.

**VARIATIONS:**

- Substitute heavy cream, cream cheese, or mascarpone and add more butter for rich mashed potatoes.

- Leave peel on and smash potatoes in the pot with a heavy object.

- Add roasted garlic or chopped fresh herbs.

# LONG-COOKED TURNIP GREENS & POT LIKKER

Greens and their pot liquid, or pot likker, are elixirs of comfort food in the South. They fix any ailment. When eaten with cornbread, they are considered a meal. Sometimes people drink the pot likker first and then eat the greens, others eat them together like a soup, and some eat the greens first, finishing with the pot likker. But the really Southern people I know dip the cornbread in the likker, getting the cornbread a bit soggy, eat it, and then follow with a bit of the turnips. Oh, but then there are those that split the cornbread and make a sandwich with the greens and a sprinkle of hot sauce in the middle. It's the combination that counts.

SERVES 6 TO 8, INCLUDING POT LIKKER

¼ pound sliced bacon, rinsed salt pork or streak o' lean, smoked neck, or other cured pork

1–2 slices onion

1 dried red chili pepper

5 pounds turnip or collard greens, washed

Salt

Freshly ground black pepper

Hot sauce, optional

Bring ½ gallon of water to the boil in a large pot over high heat. Add the pork, onion, and dried chili pepper and return to the boil. If time is available, cook to make a flavored broth, about 30 minutes.

Meanwhile, tear off and discard the stalks and any tough veins of the greens. Tear or cut the remaining greens into pieces and add to the broth. Return to the boil, reduce the heat to a simmer, pushing any bobbing greens down into the liquid, and cover. Cook 50 minutes to 3 hours, as desired. Use a pair of large scissors to cut any pieces larger than bite-sized. Taste and season with salt, pepper, and hot sauce as desired. Serve with the pot likker or strain, reserving the broth for another time. Cooked greens will last covered and refrigerated for several days. They freeze up to 3 months.

# LACY CORN FRITTERS

Served piping hot from a skillet or griddle, these crispy treasures, traditionally called hoecakes, can be thin enough to nearly see through or thick enough to dunk. With its origin perhaps in early Southern cookbooks, I've been making these with regularity since I had my restaurant in Georgia in the early 1970s. They are good by themselves, almost as a snack, or whenever cornbread would be used.

MAKES ABOUT 20 FRITTERS

9 tablespoons self-rising cornmeal mix

4 ½ tablespoons commercial or homemade self-rising flour, (page 20)

1–1 ½ cups water

½–1 teaspoon vinegary hot sauce, such as Tabasco or Texas Pete

2–4 tablespoons oil, cook's preference, for frying

Salt

Whisk together the self-rising cornmeal and flour. Add water as needed to keep batter thin, and whisk until smooth. Add hot sauce, to taste.

Heat a thin layer of oil in a large skillet over medium heat. One tablespoon at a time, drop the batter into the hot skillet. Cook each cake until brown and crisp on the bottom; turn with a spatula and then brown the other side. Add more oil to the pan as needed, and add more water to the batter as needed to keep the batter thin. Remove to a plate lined with paper towels and season with a pinch of salt just before serving.

**TIP:** If you have cornmeal that isn't self-rising, make your own by combining 9 tablespoons cornmeal with ¾ teaspoon baking powder and ¼ teaspoon salt.

# TURNIPS & CREAM AU GRATIN

Turnips enhance an au gratin with a bit of tanginess and are always available in the South in the fall. They can be layered with sliced squash or other vegetables. There is no set ratio for ingredients—and the cheese and herbs can be varied according to what is available. If only milk is available, increase the amount of butter to enrich the dish. This is a go-to Thanksgiving dish for my family, so calories don't matter, and I prepare enough for reheating leftovers. It is easily cut in half.

SERVES 10

3 pounds white turnips, peeled and sliced ⅛ inch thick

Salt

Freshly ground black pepper

2 tablespoons chopped fresh parsley, thyme and/or oregano

3 garlic cloves, finely chopped or crushed with salt

1 cup grated Gruyère cheese

1 cup freshly grated Parmesan cheese

⅓–½ cup butter

1 ½–2 cups heavy cream

½ cup breadcrumbs or panko

Bring a large pot of water to the boil, add the sliced turnips, and return to a slow boil. Simmer young and small turnips for 3 minutes and larger ones for 8 to 10 minutes to remove excess sharpness while still leaving a bit of pep in them. Drain and pat dry with paper towels.

Butter a long casserole dish, preferably no more than 3 inches deep, that will accommodate 3 layers of sliced turnips and the cheese. Spread a layer of parboiled turnips to cover the dish (they may overlap slightly) and sprinkle with salt and pepper. Mix the herbs with the garlic and sprinkle a third over the turnips. Combine the two cheeses and sprinkle the turnips with a third of the mixture. Dot with a third of the butter.

Continue to layer until all the turnips are added to the dish, finishing with cheese on top of the third layer. Pour cream over the entire dish until it barely covers the top layer of turnips. Sprinkle with the breadcrumbs or panko and dot with remaining butter. Can be made ahead to this point and refrigerated. Bring to room temperature before baking.

When ready to bake, preheat oven to 400 degrees. Add the dish, reduce the heat to 375, and bake until the cheese is melted and the breadcrumbs are nicely browned, about 45 minutes. Serve hot. This freezes up to 3 months. Defrost and reheat in a 350-degree oven for about 30 minutes, or until bubbly.

# STUFFED SQUASH & ZUCCHINI BOATS

A recipe for a stuffed vegetable can't be exact, as the vegetables vary in size. It is better to have extra stuffing than not enough, as the extra can be refrigerated or frozen for another time or baked in a ramekin for a cook's treat. This recipe will also work for those canoe-sized, end-of-season zucchini; cook both the shells and the filled zucchini a little longer.

MAKES 12, SERVES 6 TO 8

6 small zucchini or yellow squash

6 tablespoons butter, divided

1 medium onion, chopped

2 garlic cloves, chopped

1 cup grated mixed cheeses, preferably Gruyère and fresh Parmesan

3 tablespoons chopped fresh herbs such as thyme, oregano, or basil, optional, divided

Salt

Freshly ground black pepper

½ cup breadcrumbs

Preheat oven to 350 degrees.

Halve the squash and scoop out the pulp, leaving the inside walls of the vegetable intact to form boats; set aside. If any boats have broken, chop them and add to the pulp as necessary to fill the other boats. Cook the boats in the microwave until soft, just a few minutes; or slide into a pot of boiling water and cook until soft, approximately 10 minutes, remove and drain well.

Meanwhile, melt 3 tablespoons of butter in a skillet. Add the onion and any chopped squash, and cook until the onion is translucent. Add the garlic and cook a few minutes more. Cool slightly and add the cheese. Taste for seasoning, add 2 tablespoons of the herbs, if using, and season with salt and pepper.

Move the boats to a rimmed baking sheet and fill with the mixture. Top boats with breadcrumbs and dot with remaining butter. Bake until heated through, about 15 minutes. Sprinkle with remaining herbs, if using, and serve hot. May be refrigerated or frozen, wrapped well. Defrost and reheat until heated through, approximately 15 minutes.

# RATATOUILLE TIAN

Tians take simple vegetables. Combine them into an evocative design to add a touch of glamour to a meal. Have fun!

SERVES 6

1 medium onion, diced

5 garlic cloves, chopped

⅓ cup olive oil, divided

1 pint cherry tomatoes, halved

Salt

Freshly ground black pepper

2 large or 3 medium eggplants

3 medium zucchini

1 (12-ounce) jar roasted red peppers (about 2 peppers), drained and sliced

1 teaspoon chopped fresh thyme leaves, divided

1 teaspoon chopped fresh oregano, divided

¼ cup fresh basil leaves, for garnish

Preheat oven to 350.

Heat 2 tablespoons olive oil in a skillet, add onion and cook until soft, 3 to 5 minutes. Add garlic and cherry tomatoes and sauté until they begin to soften, about 5 minutes. Season with salt and pepper.

Slice eggplant and zucchini in rounds about ¼ inch thick.

To assemble the tian, overlap slices of eggplant and zucchini, alternating, around the edge of a round or oval casserole dish (about 10 inches in diameter, or a 9 x 13-inch rectangular dish). Continue with additional rows to cover the entire dish. Leave a small space open in the middle and fill with the tomato mixture. Brush the slices with 2 to 3 tablespoons olive oil. Insert red peppers strips randomly in between slices of some eggplant and zucchini. Sprinkle with thyme and oregano and season with salt and pepper.

Bake tian until vegetables are tender and juices are bubbling around the edge, about 30 to 40 minutes. Garnish with fresh basil leaves. The tian may be cooked ahead and refrigerated or frozen for reheating later. It may suffer a bit in presentation but will still be delicious.

# SOUTHERN RATATOUILLE

Meant for the time of year when the garden is brimming with an abundant mixture of vegetables, this is also highly variable. Use what's available, and don't try to be precise. If a vegetable listed is not available, omit it or add another. The vegetables are prettier and more nutritious when left unpeeled.

SERVES 10 TO 12

4 large or 6 small eggplants

Salt

3 red, yellow, or green bell peppers

6 medium zucchini

3 medium onions

8 tablespoons oil, cook's preference, divided

6 garlic cloves, chopped

2 cans Italian plum tomatoes with juice (totaling 28 ounces) or 2 pounds fresh tomatoes, chopped

1 cup chopped fresh herbs, preferably thyme, parsley, and basil

Freshly ground black pepper

Preheat oven to 350 degrees. Slice the eggplant into 1/4-inch-thick slices. Lightly score the flesh of the slices in a crosshatch pattern (like tic-tac-toe). Move slices to a colander over a bowl or sink and season with 1 teaspoon salt. Let sit 30 minutes to degorge (remove the water from) the eggplant.

Meanwhile, seed the peppers, and then slice the peppers, zucchini, and onions. Discard the liquid extracted from the eggplant. Rinse, drain, and dry eggplant well with paper towels. Brush eggplant and zucchini slices with some of the oil and move to an oiled rimmed baking sheet. Cook in the oven until lightly browned, about 20 minutes, turning halfway through.

Heat 2 tablespoons of the oil over medium high in a heavy-bottomed pan. Add the onions, peppers, and garlic, and cook until soft, adding oil as needed, about 10 minutes. Add the tomatoes and their juices and cook another 20 minutes. Add the cooked eggplant and zucchini and the herbs. Serve now, or for a thicker, softer consistency better for a bed for meats, cook another hour. Season well with black pepper. Serve hot or cold. This freezes well and reheats easily in the microwave.

# ROASTED ROOT VEGETABLES

The earthy richness of root vegetables makes them an attractive winter side dish. When I was growing up during World War Two, meat drippings were saved—usually first poured through cheesecloth to remove the cooked bits—in a metal coffee can next to the stove. When paper towels became prevalent, the can might be covered with a paper towel and secured with a sturdy rubber band and the fat poured through the towel. The drippings were mixed willy-nilly, the flavor a surprise according to the can's contents.

While drippings add an enormous amount of flavor and color, butter or oil work as well. Use as many root vegetables as available. Multicolored carrots or other vegetables add pizzazz. Turnips can be bitter if large, so if necessary, par cook as below.

SERVES 6 TO 8

3 turnips, peeled and quartered

3 medium carrots, peeled

3 medium onions, peeled

2 cups butternut squash

4–6 tablespoons drippings, cooking oil, butter, or a combination

Salt

Freshly ground black pepper

2–4 tablespoons rosemary, crumbled

Preheat oven to 400 degrees.

Cover any turnips larger than a baseball with water in a saucepan, bring to the boil, and boil 5 minutes, carefully tasting a sample before removing. (There should be no bitterness.) Drain then pat dry on paper towels.

Toss each group of vegetables in the preferred fat. Spread vegetables in one layer over a sheet pan or two, and roast in the oven until browned and crisp all over, about 1 hour, turning every 15 minutes and removing any vegetables that are cooked and browned, as they will cook according to size and density. Season with salt and pepper. Crumble rosemary on top and serve hot.

VARIATION: Add quartered fennel bulb and cook as above. Green onions and shallot bulbs can be used as well. Lemon rind and herbs are bright additions with, or instead of, the rosemary.

# LEFTOVERS

Thinking of my friend Deni Seibert causes me to tackle my fridge after holidays. It is typically crammed full of various leftovers—some watercress and turnip greens flavored with meaty ham hocks, in broth as solid as Jell-O; a few bits of turkey in the broth from the boiled-down carcass; green onion tops whose bulbs had seen better days; several very ripe tomatoes; a hard piece of cheddar; some candied fruit and cream cheese.

Deni has perfected her leftovers into an art in the form of weekly made soup. Russ, her husband, was director of Longwood Gardens in Delaware for years, and they brought their children up there. Deni has the ability never to be flustered, even when the doorbell rings and some person, perhaps never met before but heard about, is at her door saying, "I know this is rude, but I've wanted to meet you for ever so long and found that I had just enough time before going to the airport if I drove straight here without calling and rang your doorbell." Deni brings them into her kitchen, makes them feel completely at ease, and, if they are very lucky, they get her homemade soup.

She starts a new soup fresh each week, beginning with the Sunday meal's leftovers—a ham bone boiled up, or the bone from whatever meat she served for Sunday dinner. Each day through the rest of the week, leftovers are added to her soup. The best day is Saturday. By that time the soup is chock-full of surprises—carrots from Wednesday, butter beans from Thursday, a couple of cut-up boiled potatoes from Friday. Perhaps it is easy to be gracious if you always know you have a good soup in the fridge.

The truth is, anyone can make a soup with the bits and pieces one has in the fridge. It is good to start with a broth to give the soup body. If you have a chicken or duck or turkey carcass with a little meat still clinging to the bones, you have a fine base. Better still if you have some ham hocks in jelly. If you cut up your own raw chickens every time you're preparing fried chicken or a sauté, it is provident to save the backbone, neck, and gizzards, and package and freeze them until you have enough packages for a stock.

When preparing vegetables, I chuck into a freezer bag the end pieces of onions and carrots and maybe other vegetables, as well as parsley stalks, outer ribs of celery, and so on, and these all go into the soup pot. (I'm afraid I save the green onion tops for myself and char them until crisp—a cook's treat.)

But to get back to the findings in my own post-holiday fridge: in addition to making a turkey and/or ham soup, I can use up two leftover tortillas! I'll use the tomatoes in a tomato bruschetta with some slightly stale Italian bread I have on hand. The bit of cheese has a speck of mold on it, but that doesn't hurt cheese. I'll just scrape it off and use it along with the leftover meat on the ham hocks to make a gougère— that delicious French cheesy cream puff that my nearly-daughter Audrey and her Frenchman beau taught me how to put together (they'll often make an entire meal of a gougère). The leftover vegetables will also work nicely cooked together. And that eggplant can make a nice snacking appetizer, too, while I wait.

Finally, there's the candied fruit and some cream cheese. Almond crisp cookies are a good solution for leftover candied fruit, but then I also remember a recipe from Betty Rosbottom for a wonderful cheesecake that uses both candied fruit and cream cheese—and a fair amount of sour cream, I admit—but better to add to what I have and produce a scrumptious dessert than to throw away any usable ingredient. Now I've made a clean sweep. What a feeling of satisfaction!

# CELERY & CARROTS WITH GINGER SAUCE

Rather than needing a separate pan, the ginger sauce makes itself from the vegetables mixed with the seasonings. For that reason, the heat should be kept low enough to have the vegetables extrude their juices. Too high a heat will cause them to evaporate and be sauceless, but they will still be delicious.

SERVES 4

6 tablespoons butter

8 stalks celery, sliced on the diagonal (about 2 cups)

4 large carrots, sliced on the diagonal (about 2 cups)

¼ cup granulated sugar

1 ½–3 teaspoons chopped fresh ginger

1 handful small fresh mint leaves, about ⅓ cup

Melt the butter over low heat in a heavy pan. Add the celery and carrots. Cover and cook over low heat until barely crunchy, about 10 minutes. Mix together the sugar and ginger in a small bowl and add to the pan. Stir the celery and carrots in the sugar-ginger mixture slowly and gently until they are well glazed and slightly browned. If the mint leaves aren't small and pretty, chop coarsely; otherwise leave them whole. Dish up, stirring in the mint.

**VARIATION:** Cook in a skillet for more tender-crisp vegetables, or cook in a pot for longer to yield softer vegetables.

# PAN-CHARRED GREEN BEANS WITH PECANS

This has been a favorite recipe of mine since a brief stint living in New York in the Village. I was out of butter and asked my beau to bring some to flavor the green beans when cooked. I added the beans to boiling salted water and carelessly left the pan uncovered while I stepped out of the kitchen. The liquid quickly boiled out, and I returned to charred beans. I tasted them, and they were delicious, and voila! A recipe was born! I realized I did not need water or fat to cook the green beans and liked them charred and slightly crunchy. The pecans only made it better, as did the butter when it arrived.

An under-salted green bean is worse than an undercooked one. Be sure to taste and season as needed.

SERVES 4

3 tablespoons butter, divided

1 pound green beans, ends and strings removed

Salt

½ cup chopped pecans

Freshly ground black pepper

Heat a large cast-iron or heavy-duty skillet over high heat. Add 1 tablespoon of the butter. Add the green beans in one layer to the hot skillet. Sprinkle 1 teaspoon salt over the beans. Cook over high heat, tossing occasionally. Add butter only if they start to stick. Toss the beans occasionally and continue to cook until blistered with occasional charring, about 5 minutes. When cooked, remove beans to a plate. Melt any additional butter in the skillet and sauté chopped pecans until toasty. Return cooked green beans to the skillet and toss with buttered pecans to combine. Season with salt and pepper to taste.

# SOCIAL CIRCLE MACARONI PIE

Celeste Dupree, maven of Social Circle, Georgia, taught me how important Macaroni Pie is to the South when she taught me to make this custardy rendition of macaroni and cheese. I use it as a side dish, a starter, or a main course. It can be doubled if a larger dish is used. It is an ultimate comfort food.

SERVES 6-8

3 cups cooked and drained spaghetti (macaroni)

4 tablespoons butter, melted

4 large eggs, beaten to mix

3 cups milk

1 1/2 teaspoons Dijon mustard

2 teaspoons salt

Freshly ground black pepper

1 teaspoon ground hot red pepper, optional

1 pound sharp cheddar or Gruyère cheese, grated

Preheat oven to 350 degrees.

Roughly cut the cooked spaghetti into 3-inch pieces and toss with half the butter. Lightly whisk the eggs with the milk in a large bowl. Add the mustard, salt, peppers, and half the cheese. Put half the spaghetti into a greased 3-quart baking dish, sprinkle with cheese to cover and 1 tablespoon of the butter. Ladle on half the egg/cheese mixture, top with the rest of the spaghetti. Ladle on the remainder of the mixture and enough cheese and the remaining butter to cover the top. If the dish is deep, it may not need all the cheese.

Move to the preheated oven. If the dish is less than three inches deep, bake for 30 minutes; if deeper, bake for about 45 minutes. Check and reduce the heat 25 degrees if the cheese is browning too much or the custard is bubbling. Cover lightly with foil and continue to cook until a fork inserted in the custard comes out clean and the top is golden brown, up to 40 minutes more, depending on the thickness of the baking dish.

# DESSERTS

Desserts are my downfall. I truly love desserts as much as savory dishes. My favorite is a batter cobbler, in part because the grandchildren love it so. A single cobbler can be eaten by six people or two, with the two people eating it again for a slightly sinful breakfast and maybe for lunch as well. But I long for meringues, as they make me think of my childhood when I loved making them. And how could I leave out a croquembouche, which brings to mind the glorious dessert served for my oldest "nearly" daughter, Audrey, and her husband, Pierre-Henri, at their wedding supper. Made of little puffs that look like small cabbages and taste divine with their fillings of flavored creams and topped with little wisps of caramel—well, of course I dream of them. There is the chocolate snowball, that old workhorse of a dessert, made so simply and stunning the diners with its deliciousness and beauty. How could I give it up?

The caramel cake is another I dream about, remembering MaMa Dupree's efforts to please us with one, so many years ago, and craving it whenever I think of good cooking. I hope you think of me as you cook these recipes, and make them your favorites too.

# LAZY GIRL PEACH BATTER COBBLER

This cakey cobbler is a Southern standby. In Social Circle, Georgia, where I lived for many years, this was a frequent favorite at church and potluck suppers. Our grandchildren expect me to bring it when we join them at the beach or when they come to our home, in which case I double the recipe—because it also happens to be delicious for breakfast.

SERVES 4 TO 6

1 cup granulated sugar, divided

2 cups sliced peaches

½ cup unsalted butter

1 cup commercial or homemade self-rising flour, (page 20)

1 cup whole milk

Sprinkle ¼ cup of the sugar over the peaches and let sit while melting the butter. In an 8 x 11-inch baking dish or decorative oven-to-table dish, melt butter in the oven while the oven preheats to 375 degrees. (The butter crisps the edges, so I say "the bigger the dish, the better." If you prefer a deeper cobbler, use a smaller baking dish.)

Whisk together the flour, milk, and remaining sugar. It can be just a bit lumpy. When the butter has melted, remove the hot pan and pour the batter into the hot butter in the pan. Don't worry if the batter puffs up a bit on the sides. Sprinkle the peaches evenly over the top of the batter.

Bake until the batter has risen around the fruit, the top is light brown and "cobbled" looking, and the sides are darker brown, about 30 to 45 minutes. An inserted fork should come out clean. Serve hot. It can be made ahead and refrigerated or frozen. Reheat before serving.

**VARIATIONS:**

- Brown sugar can be used instead of granulated sugar. It makes a less crisp cobbler.

- Bake in a well-seasoned iron skillet. Turn out baked cobbler upside down onto a separate serving dish or platter.

- Frozen peaches or other frozen fruit can be substituted.

- Finely chopped crystalized ginger is a lovely addition.

# FREE-FORM PEAR TART

The sinuousness of the vertically sliced pears makes a stunning presentation, but sliced apples and peaches hold their own as well. Drain any excess liquid before arranging on the piecrust. If the pears are soft, slice them a little thicker.

SERVES 4 TO 6

1 recipe Very Versatile Cream Cheese Dough (page 160), or 1 (9-inch) store-bought piecrust

2–3 Bosc or other cooking pears, cored and sliced vertically ¼-inch thick

½ cup granulated sugar, divided

Chopped candied ginger, optional

1 large egg mixed with 1 tablespoon water

2 tablespoons apricot jelly, warmed in microwave

Preheat oven to 375 degrees. Line a baking sheet with parchment paper. Roll the piecrust into a round ⅛-inch thick, or any desired shape. Set on top of the parchment-lined baking sheet and chill 30 minutes. Toss the fruit slices with ¼ cup of the granulated sugar. Leaving a 1-inch border around the edge of the crust, arrange the pear slices neatly into a circular fan pattern, making about two to three concentric circles. Make an edge and fold the 1-inch border up over the pears, if necessary, on all sides to make a rim to contain the mixture, pleating every inch or so to maintain the shape. Sprinkle remaining sugar, and candied ginger if using, over the top of the pears. Refrigerate at least 15 minutes, or as necessary to chill the dough.

Move the baking sheet to the preheated oven and bake for 20 minutes. Remove from the oven, brush the edges with the egg wash, reduce oven temperature to 350 degrees, and bake until crust is golden brown, about an additional 10 minutes. If using peaches or apples it may require a bit more time to brown. Remove the tart carefully using two spatulas to a wire rack to cool. Brush the top with 2 tablespoons warm apricot jelly. Serve at room temperature.

**VARIATIONS:**

• Lemon zest and/or cinnamon sugar are child-pleasing additions for winter nights.

• Shape into a long rectangle or cut into hearts or other shapes for individual servings.

# LEMON & BERRY TART

Lemon curd and berries are a classic combination, with the curd made in advance and the berries added a few hours before serving. As a general rule, I taste any fruit I use in a recipe but especially berries, which can range in sweetness, adding powdered sugar if needed. Lemon juices vary in tartness.

If the curd is too tart, dust with powdered sugar before serving. When in a hurry, this can be made with a store-bought crust. I prefer the national brand that comes two rolled doughs to a box.

MAKES 1 9-INCH TART

1 recipe Lemon Curd, see page 159

1 recipe Very Versatile Cream Cheese Dough (page 160), or 1 (9-inch) store-bought piecrust, rolled to 1/8-to-1/4-inch thickness

2–3 cups fresh berries, such as raspberries, blueberries, or strawberries

Confectioners' sugar, optional

Prepare the Lemon Curd as directed on page 159, and chill. Preheat oven to 350 degrees.

Arrange the piecrust in a 9-inch tart pan, preferably with a removable bottom, cutting off any excess. Lightly prick the surface of the piecrust with the tines of a fork. Crumple a piece of parchment, waxed paper, or aluminum foil. Reopen, smooth out, and place into the piecrust and fill with raw rice, beans, or pie weights. Bake until the piecrust is fully cooked, about 25 minutes, covering edges as necessary to prevent burning. Remove from oven, scoop out the pie weights, remove paper, and let cool on a rack. When cool, remove outer ring of tart pan, fill crust with lemon curd, smoothing the top with an offset spatula or knife. Arrange berries in a pattern on curd as desired. Chill before serving. Dust with confectioners' sugar, if desired.

**VARIATION:** Make into bite-sized or individual tarts or as a prebaked, free-form tart (page 156).

> CONTINUED

# LEMON CURD

Curd is an indelicate way to describe this smooth, creamy lemon sauce, which goes back in time to old and modern French, English, and Southern recipes, including Thomas Jefferson's and Martha Washington's collections. The curd itself is delicious as a filling for cakes, meringues, tarts, and pies. It can be made with a whole egg instead of yolks, but care must be taken to avoid overcooking the whites; so I stick with yolks and use the whites for another purpose. My friend and coauthor Cynthia has made it in a slow cooker with a whole egg.

Like mayonnaise, lemon curd will last a long time in the refrigerator, as it has a high degree of acid (a low pH). If mixed with something that dilutes the acidity, its life span is shortened. Since citrus acidity varies and the home cook has no real idea of its strength, some care should be taken. Usually it can be kept, tightly sealed and refrigerated, for up to a month.

MAKES 2 ½ CUPS

5 large egg yolks

1 cup granulated sugar

½ cup unsalted butter, softened

½ cup fresh lemon juice

3 tablespoons lemon rind, no white attached

Lightly whisk the egg yolks in a heavy saucepan, bowl, bain-marie, or double boiler. Whisk in the sugar and butter, then the lemon juice.

Stir the egg mixture with a rubber spatula over low heat until thick but still falling easily from a spoon, 5 to 10 minutes, making sure to scrape the sides and bottom occasionally. The temperature should register approximately 170 degrees and it should be saucy. If too thin, carefully cook a few minutes longer. (If the mixture simmers at the edges of the pan, quickly strain; it will be usable if smooth and no egg bits remain.)

Add the rind to the egg mixture. Taste for flavor and add more juice or rind if necessary and available. Remove from the heat and cool. Store in the refrigerator in a tightly covered jar.

N O T E :  Peculiarly, egg yolks do not like sugar sitting on top of them without any agitation from a spoon or whisk. The sugar tends to "cook" the egg yolk.

> CONTINUED

**VARIATIONS:**

- For a faster sauce, spread sugar out on a half-sheet pan and heat at 400 degrees before adding.

- To lighten the lemon curd, fold in whipped cream, mascarpone, or meringue before serving.

- Lime, orange, and other citrus juices, as well as cooked caramelized pineapple, are wonderful variations. Adjust the amount of juice as needed, keeping in mind that acid is necessary for thickening the mixture and to lower the pH.


# VERY VERSATILE
# CREAM CHEESE DOUGH

This is a miracle dough, adapted from one of Rose Beranbaum's recipes in her book *The Pastry Bible*. It is most easily made in a food processor or mixer but can be made by hand. It is flaky and tender and browns beautifully. The cream cheese emulsifies, tenderizes, and is pretty indestructible. The only moment of trickiness is rolling out the dough, as it wants to stick and pull apart. This doesn't hurt the dough, as it can be pushed back together, but it is a bit alarming when it first happens. Rolling the dough between pieces of plastic wrap or in a large plastic bag eases the anxiety. The recipe can be easily doubled.

MAKES 1 (9-INCH) PIECRUST OR 30 TO 40 TASSIES

1 ½ cups all-purpose flour, preferably soft-wheat, divided

½ cup unsalted butter, cut into ½-inch cubes and frozen

3 ounces cream cheese, cut into 4 pieces and chilled (not frozen)

1 large egg mixed with 1 tablespoon water, to glaze


Before measuring, whisk flour in its container with a wire whisk or fork to lighten. Take a large spoon and scoop up the flour from the container and slide it into a dry measuring cup. When full, level off any excess flour with the back of a knife. Add 1 cup of the flour to the bowl of a food processor. Set aside remaining ½ cup flour for rolling out the dough.

Add the butter cubes to the food processor and pulse until the size of oatmeal or grits. Add the cream cheese pieces and pulse quickly until it becomes a lumpy dough. Scrape out the dough between two pieces of plastic wrap or onto a large plastic bag. Press dough into a smooth, flat disc about 8 inches in diameter. Move dough to a clean plastic bag or wrap in plastic, and refrigerate at least 30 minutes or up to 5 days.

Roll out the pastry into a ⅛-inch-thick round between two pieces of plastic wrap or in a large plastic bag. If sticky, sprinkle the surface with a bit of the remaining flour. If using a tart pan with removable bottom, surround the bottom and sides of the pan tightly with foil to prevent filling from leaking out while baking. Remove the top sheet of plastic wrap or slit the bag and flip dough into a pie or tart pan. Fit dough into the recesses of the pan by lifting gently and lightly pressing dough along the bottom and sides of pan. Remove second sheet of plastic wrap. Decorate edges as desired. Prick the bottoms and sides lightly with a fork. Chill 30 minutes or more, or freeze if desired.

When ready to use, preheat oven to 350 degrees. Crumple a piece of parchment, waxed paper, or aluminum foil; reopen, smooth out, and place into the piecrust. Fill with raw rice, beans, or pie weights and prebake 15 minutes, covering edges as necessary to prevent burning. A roasting bag, as used for roasting chicken, is an ideal substitute for the paper. It can be filled with rice and beans or weights, put on the crust, removed, and reused at a later time.

Remove crust from oven, scoop out rice and beans, remove paper, and brush bottom with egg glaze. Reduce the heat to 300 degrees and return to oven until completely baked, about 6 to 8 minutes. Remove from oven, cool on a rack, and fill as desired.

# ROSE'S BEST
# ALL-AMERICAN APPLE PIE

Rose Beranbaum has been a long-time culinary hero of mine. I read her books and follow her blog. She is doggedly precise enough to ensure success to all. She has a chart in her book *The Pastry Bible* for the best apples to use for baking.

MAKES 1 (9-INCH) DOUBLE-CRUST PIE

2 batches Very Versatile Cream Cheese Dough (page 160), kept separate

Extra all-purpose flour for rolling

2 ½ pounds baking apples, such as Golden Delicious or Galas, peeled, cored, and sliced ¼-inch thick (about 4–6 apples, 8 cups sliced)

1 tablespoon lemon juice

¼ cup packed light brown sugar

¼ cup granulated sugar

¾ teaspoon ground cinnamon

¼ teaspoon freshly grated nutmeg

¼ teaspoon salt

2 tablespoons unsalted butter

1 tablespoon + 1 teaspoon cornstarch

Remove one dough for the bottom crust from the refrigerator. If necessary, allow it to sit for about 10 minutes or until it is soft enough to roll.

On a floured pastry cloth or between two sheets of lightly floured plastic wrap, roll the bottom crust ⅛ inch thick or less and 12 inches in diameter. Transfer it to the pie pan. Trim the edge almost even with the edge of the pan. Cover with plastic wrap and refrigerate for a minimum of 30 minutes and a maximum of 3 hours.

In a large bowl, combine the apples, lemon juice, sugars, cinnamon, nutmeg, and salt and toss to mix. Allow the apples to macerate at room temperature for a minimum of 30 minutes and a maximum of 3 hours.

Transfer the apples and their juices to a colander suspended over a bowl to capture the liquid. The mixture will release at least ½ cup of liquid.

In a small saucepan (preferably nonstick), over medium-high heat, boil down this liquid, with the butter, to about ⅓ cup (a little more if you started with more than ½ cup of liquid), or until syrupy and lightly caramelized. Swirl the liquid but do not stir it. (Alternatively, spray a heatproof 4-cup measuring cup with nonstick vegetable spray, add the liquid and butter, and boil it in the microwave 6 to 7 minutes on high.) Meanwhile, transfer apples to a bowl and toss with the cornstarch until all traces of it have disappeared.

Pour the syrup over the apples, tossing gently. (Do not be concerned if the liquid hardens on contact with the apples; it will dissolve during baking.)

Roll out the second dough for the top crust, large enough to cut a 12-inch circle. Use an expandable flan ring or a cardboard template and a sharp knife as a cutting guide.

Transfer apple mixture to the pie shell. Moisten the border of the bottom crust by brushing it lightly with water then place the top crust over the fruit. Tuck the overhang under the bottom crust border and press down all around the top to seal it. Crimp the border using a fork or your fingers, and make about 5 evenly spaced 2-inch slashes in the top, starting about 1 inch from the center and radiating toward the edge. Cover the pie loosely with plastic wrap and refrigerate for 1 hour to chill and relax the pastry. This will maintain flakiness and help to keep the crust from shrinking while baking.

Preheat the oven to 425 at least 20 minutes before baking. Set an oven rack at the lowest level and place a baking stone or baking sheet on it before preheating. Place a large piece of greased foil on top to catch any juices.

Set the pie directly on the foil-topped baking stone and bake for 45 to 55 minutes, or until the juices bubble through the slashes and the apples feel tender but not mushy when a cake tester or small sharp knife is inserted through a slash. After 30 minutes, protect the edges from over-browning with a foil ring.

Cool the pie on a rack for at least 4 hours before cutting, as it will be gooey. Serve warm or at room temperature. Store at room temperature up to 3 days.

> CONTINUED

# APPLE ROSES

My once apprentice Nicole Mariner first showed me how to make these little roses. I fell in love with them and now make them whenever I can. To start, learn using a name-brand boxed pie-crust and then move to your own if you prefer. And of course, made from any leftover dough, they can be the cook's treat.

MAKES ABOUT 10

2 Gala or other red-skinned apples

¼ cup granulated sugar

Pinch salt

¼ teaspoon cinnamon, optional

½ teaspoon lemon zest, optional

1 (9-inch) piecrust

Flour for rolling

1 teaspoon cinnamon sugar, optional

Preheat oven to 350 degrees. Grease a mini-muffin tin and set aside.

Wash the apples and remove cores, but do not peel them. The skin is what gives the roses their red color. Cut apples in half from stem to blossom end. Slice each half into very thin wedges, about 1/8-inch thick. In a microwaveable bowl, stir together sugar, salt, and optional cinnamon and lemon zest. Add apple slices and stir to coat. Microwave for 45 seconds to 1 minute, until apples are tender and pliable. Allow to cool.

Place the piecrust on a lightly floured surface and roll out until about 1/8 inch thick. Cut into ten 1½ x 6-inch strips. Arrange about 6 to 8 apple slices lengthwise across the top of the strip of dough, rounded skin-side up, overlapping slightly. Fold up the bottom half of the dough and press to enclose the apples. Gently, tightly roll the dough to form a rose shape. Wet your fingers with the juices from the cooked apples to help seal the dough; place in the muffin tin. Then repeat with remaining dough and apples. Sprinkle with cinnamon sugar and bake in preheated oven for about 20 to 25 minutes, until pie dough is cooked and roses are golden brown. Allow to cool for a few minutes, then remove the roses to a cooling rack.

**VARIATION:** There are various jelly glazes that spruce up pies and tarts. The rule of thumb is that red fruit should have a red glaze. Heat red currant, mixed berry, or other red jam or jelly with a small amount of water in a small saucepan over low heat to thin; strain if necessary, then brush on while pie dough and jelly are both hot. For yellow fruits, we use a clear or light-colored jam such as apricot, orange marmalade, pineapple, etc.

# PECAN TASSIES

Tassies are miniature Southern tarts, typically served at bridal showers, weddings, or any time a special little-sized delicacy is needed. They are the cook's hidden weapon, as they freeze so nicely and can be made well in advance. The Very Versatile Cream Cheese Dough is easily pushed into the tiny tins. Pecans have a certain affection for bourbon, but vanilla is also a good addition.

MAKES 30 TO 40 TASSIES

1 recipe Very Versatile Cream Cheese Dough, page 160

1 large egg

½ cup packed light or dark brown sugar (use ¾ cup for a sweeter filling)

1 tablespoon unsalted butter, melted

1 teaspoon bourbon extract, bourbon, or vanilla extract

⅛ teaspoon salt

⅔ cup chopped pecans, divided

Prepare the Very Versatile Cream Cheese Dough as directed. Divide dough into 30 equal pieces and roll to make little balls. Chill the balls for 30 minutes or up to several days.

Move the balls to 30 tiny, lightly greased, fluted mini tart pans or miniature muffin cups on a rimmed baking sheet. Press the dough balls with fingertips or a tart tamper (a wooden dowel that comes with different-sized rounded ends) against the bottoms and sides. Move baking sheets with the lined pans to the refrigerator or freezer to chill while preparing the filling. If any tassies crack after refrigeration, press a small amount of dough onto the crack to cover.

Preheat oven to 325 degrees. Beat together the egg, brown sugar, butter, extract, and salt in a mixing bowl until all the lumps are gone. Line the dough-lined pans with half the pecans and carefully spoon in the egg mixture, taking care to keep the filling below the sides of the dough, thus preventing it from slipping under the dough and caramelizing, making it difficult to remove the tassie. Dot with the remaining pecans. Bake until the filling is set, about 25 minutes. Cool 5 minutes on a rack, making sure to remove tassies from the pans while they are still warm lest they stick. If tassies are reluctant to come out, insert a small thin knife between the tassie and the pan and give the tassie a boost.

These will keep several days closely wrapped or 3 months in the freezer. They defrost quickly at room temperature or can be heated on a rimmed baking sheet while still frozen.

**VARIATION: CHOCOLATE PECAN TASSIES**

Add 1/3 cup miniature chocolate chips to the recipe, putting half into the tins with half of the pecans. Dot the filled tins with the remaining half of the chips and nuts.

# LEMON TASSIES

MAKES ABOUT 30

1 recipe Very Versatile Cream Cheese Dough
  (page 160)

1 recipe Lemon Curd (page 159)

1 large egg mixed with 1 tablespoon water,
  to glaze

Prepare the Very Versatile Cream Cheese Dough as directed (page 160). Divide the dough into 30 equal pieces and roll into balls. Chill the balls for 30 minutes. Meanwhile, prepare the Lemon Curd as directed (page 159). Chill at least 1 hour.

Move the balls to 30 tiny, lightly greased, fluted mini tart pans or miniature muffin cups placed on a rimmed baking sheet. Press the dough with fingertips or a tart tamper (a wooden dowel that comes with different-sized rounded ends) against the bottoms and sides. Place the baking sheets with the lined pans in the refrigerator to chill for 30 minutes. If any tarts crack after refrigeration, press a small amount of dough onto the crack to cover.

Preheat oven to 350 degrees. Crumple several small pieces of parchment, waxed paper, or aluminum foil; reopen, smooth out, and place into the tiny crusts; fill with raw rice, beans, or pie weights and prebake 15 minutes, covering edges as necessary to prevent burning. Remove from oven, scoop out rice and beans, remove paper, and brush bottom with egg glaze. Reduce the heat to 300 degrees and return to the oven for 6 to 8 minutes, or until completely baked. Remove from oven, cool on a rack, and fill with chilled Lemon Curd.

**VARIATIONS:** Top tarts with a blueberry, raspberry, or curled lemon rind or other garnish. Or fill any empty tarts with a good-quality, delicious fruit jam.

# CHOCOLATE SNOWBALL

Our snow is as light as this layer of snowy white whipping cream covering a dense chocolate ball as big as a glass bowl. It is as easy to serve and cut as a cake and even easier to make using a food processor or mixer. Having arrived in the South from the North, this recipe is here to stay. The recipe doubles easily, making one gigantic ball or two dinner party-sized ones. It is a perfect Passover dessert as it contains no flour.

SERVES 6 TO 8

1 (12-ounce) package semisweet chocolate chips

½ cup water

1 cup plus 2 tablespoons granulated sugar, divided

1 cup unsalted butter, room temperature

4 large eggs

1 tablespoon vanilla extract, optional

1 cup heavy cream

1 teaspoon vanilla extract

Grated chocolate for garnish, optional

Preheat oven to 350 degrees. Line a 5-cup ovenproof bowl with a double thickness of foil.

Melt the chocolate with the water and 1 cup sugar over low heat or in the microwave; cool slightly. Transfer the chocolate mixture to a mixing bowl or food processor bowl fitted with the metal blade. Beat in the butter then add the eggs one by one, beating after each addition. Stir in the vanilla.

Pour the mixture into the foil-lined mold. Bake until a thick crust has formed on top, about 1 to 1½ hours. It will still be soft, lightly jiggly, and slightly wet under the crust.

Remove from oven. It will collapse. Cool completely. Cover tightly and refrigerate until solid, 2 to 3 hours or overnight, or freeze. This can be done several days in advance.

When ready to serve, whip the cream with 2 tablespoons sugar and vanilla until stiff. Cut a small slit in one corner of a plastic bag, or use a plastic or pastry bag with a tip. Position the bag in a sturdy mug or glass, and fold the top third of the bag down around the outside of the container. Scoop the cream from the bowl into the bag until it is half full. Pull up the surrounding part of the bag and twist

> CONTINUED

the cream-free top to keep the cream from gushing out. Hold the twisted part of the bag with the dominant hand, and position the fingers of the other hand at the bottom tip. When ready to pipe, push from the top.

Remove the snowball from the bowl and peel off the foil. Place on a serving dish, flat side down.

Pipe rosettes of whipped cream over the entire surface until no chocolate shows and it looks like a snowball. Chill until served. Press grated chocolate through a sieve over the piped cream, if desired. Slice in wedges to serve. Leftovers freeze well, tightly wrapped—good enough for family anyway.

**VARIATIONS:**

- Bake in a 3-to-4-inch-deep springform pan with a removable bottom. When cooked, remove, decorate the sides and rim with whipped cream, and serve as a cake and call it something else. Timing will vary.

- For individual servings, bake in smaller dishes, but watch timing carefully, as it varies with the size of the dish.

# TRADITIONAL SIMPLE MERINGUES

Meringues are fun to make and shape, both in traditional and whimsical ways. When the seasons change, I move from meringue baskets holding fruit, lemon curd, or cream, to pillows—sometimes raspberry pillows. I then move to Mont Blancs, tiny snowman-shaped meringues—and even teardrops dipped in chocolate. They are inexpensive to make, so experimenting is permissible. A little warning: muggy and humid or rainy days create some problems for meringue-making. Bake them at a lower heat, or turn heat down if they start to darken, and bake longer.

MAKES 30 TO 35

4 egg whites, room temperature (4 ounces)

¼ teaspoon cream of tartar

½ teaspoon salt

1 cup granulated sugar

¼–½ teaspoon vanilla extract

Preheat oven to 200 degrees. Oil and flour one or two rimmed baking sheets. Line with parchment or waxed paper, and oil and flour the paper. (This makes cleanup much easier.) The pans should be no longer than the length from the back of the oven to the front when the door is closed. If the pans are larger and only fit across the oven, halve the recipe, using just one pan rather than setting one pan directly under the other or letting the meringue mixture sit more than an hour while the first batch dries.

Beat the egg whites in a large bowl using a stand mixer fitted with a rotary whisk, or an electric hand mixer, or by hand with a balloon whisk, starting slowly and increasing speed until they are foamy. Add the cream of tartar and salt, then continue beating, gradually increasing the speed (it gets easier to beat as the pockets of air form) just until soft peaks form and the egg whites barely slide in the bowl when tipped. Avoid letting them get "rocky" looking and overbeaten.

Beat in half the sugar 1 tablespoon at a time, and continue beating until the meringue is very stiff and shiny. Sprinkle remaining sugar on top, add vanilla, and fold in with a metal spoon or rubber spatula, using a figure-eight motion to go down to the bottom of the pan and back up again, rotating the bowl after each "eight." If the meringue deflates, beat further by hand with a balloon whisk to make firm peaks. An extra egg white will save overbeaten rocky egg whites. Beat in as needed.

> CONTINUED

**SHAPING AND BAKING MERINGUES**: To make cloud shapes, dump a spoonful of meringue onto the paper and make a little depression with the back of the spoon that will be deep enough to hold cream and berries; repeat to fill the pan. Different-sized spoons will produce different-sized meringues, which requires an adjustment in time of baking. Bake 1 to 3 hours at 200 degrees to dry the meringues.

To make rounds to sandwich fillings like whipped cream or lemon curd, with or without fruit, draw circles on the paper. Spoon the meringue into the rounds evenly so they will stack when dried.

To pipe the meringue, cut a small slit in one corner of a plastic bag or use a plastic or pastry bag with a tip. Position the bag in a sturdy mug or glass, and fold the top third of the bag down around the outside of the container. Scoop the meringue from the bowl into the bag until it is half full. Pull up the surrounding part of the bag and twist the meringue-free top to keep the meringue from gushing out. Hold the twisted part of the bag with the dominant hand, and position the fingers of the other hand at the bottom tip, avoiding putting a hand (which is hot and will melt the sugar) on the side of the bag. Push from the top.

For traditional kiss-sized meringues, guide the bag with the fingers to the top of the pan, push gently from the top of the bag onto the pan and make a small round. Lift the bag, pulling up to make a point on the top of the meringue, and stop pushing.

To make larger, "two-bump" meringues, push from the top onto the pan, making a much larger bottom round. Pull up slightly, releasing, then push down again, making a second smaller bump, and pull up to make a point on the top.

To bake meringues, put the first tray vertically into a preheated 200-degree oven on the top shelf without touching the sides of the oven. Fill the second tray, as above, and move down a rack and to the other side of the oven, staggering the pans so the air can circulate around them. This will prevent the meringues on the top and bottom rows from overbrowning when the heat hits and the air can't circulate.

**TIPS:** Leftover and crumbled meringue mixed with whipped cream and a sauce or purée, such as lemon curd or raspberry purée, can be served as is or chilled and frozen in a plastic-lined loaf pan. Freeze, remove, and slice to serve.

Since the ratio of 2 portions of sugar to 1 portion of egg white is the same no matter how many eggs are whipped, the recipe works as well with larger or smaller amounts.

# SWISS MERINGUES

This meringue recipe produces a more stable, "brighter white" meringue as a result of cooking the egg white to 120 degrees before baking. I find that measuring the sugar onto a piece of waxed paper or parchment makes it easy to add with one hand while beating with the other. Ingredients are the same as for Traditional Simple Meringues.

MAKES 30 TO 35

4 egg whites, room temperature (4 ounces)

¼ teaspoon cream of tartar

½ teaspoon salt

1 cup granulated sugar

¼–½ teaspoon vanilla extract

Oil and flour the baking pans. Whisk the egg whites in a large bowl using a stand mixer fitted with a rotary whisk, or an hand mixer, or by hand with a balloon whisk, starting slowly, until they are foamy. Add the cream of tartar and the salt and continue, gradually increasing speed, until they form very soft peaks and barely slide in the bowl. Move the bowl over a pan of simmering water and steadily whisk in the sugar. Add the vanilla. Continue whisking until the mixture forms a glossy stiff peak and does not slide in the bowl, about 5 minutes by mixer, longer by hand. The mixture needs to register 120 degrees on a thermometer. If beaten too long, it looks rocky and starts to separate. If that happens, remove from the heat and continue whisking until the meringue is cool. Shape and bake as on page 174.

**TIP:** For an even more stable meringue, preheat oven to 400 degrees. Spread superfine sugar out on a parchment-lined half sheet pan and bake sugar for 3 minutes stirring after a minute or two. Do not let caramelize unintentionally. Pile up a small amount of the sugar, insert a thermometer, and remove the pan when the temperature is 220 degrees.

Using the parchment as a funnel, steadily whisk the still hot sugar to the beaten egg whites when moving the bowl over simmering water as above.

**VARIATION: JAM-SWIRLED MERINGUE PILLOWS**

A fruit jam can be swirled into the meringue just before baking to give added color and flavor. Prepare the Swiss Meringue as directed. Heat ¼ cup jam of your choice in the microwave for about 20 to 30 seconds to loosen. (Dark red raspberry works well for its bold color.) Pour through a fine mesh sieve into a small bowl. There are also commercial packaged sauces found in pastry aisles that can be used.

Just before shaping your meringues, dollop a couple of tablespoons of prepared jam over the top of the batter. Gently swirl jam through the meringue with one or two strokes of a spatula. Using a large serving spoon, scoop about ½ cup meringue and dollop gently onto the prepared baking sheet; use a second large spoon to help coax the meringue from the spoon, swirling the jam throughout the meringue with a small flourish as it drops. Bake as directed until dry, about 2 to 3 hours in a 200-degree oven.

## SEPARATING EGGS

Hit egg lightly but firmly on the counter or table. Using both hands, separate shell halves. Capture the yolk with one hand and let the rest slide into the bowl through the fingers of the other. Move egg yolk to one bowl, egg white to a larger one. Crack the next egg into a third bowl and move white and yolk once separated into the established bowls. The egg whites should be free of any yolk, which prevents them from beating. One egg white from a grade A large egg is a bit over one liquid ounce.

# MERINGUES REMIND ME OF PARIS

Meringues have been my comfort food since I was old enough to beat an egg white. In those days I beat them using a rotary hand whisk, a less-than-ideal solution but all I knew. I would work and work, turning the handle, watching the eggs gather and thicken in the too-small bowl. My spindly arms, unused to such activity, would give out after half an hour or so. I would add all the sugar at once and usually wind up with a thick, sugary mess. Disheartened, I would spread it out in dollops on a greased steel baking sheet and put them in a low oven, hoping for the best. Then I would go read my favorite books, *Heidi, Heidi Grows Up*, and *Heidi's Children*, in the corner of the living room behind a big red easy chair, and wait.

Decades later, I associate meringues with Paris and Angelina's Restaurant on the rue de Rivoli, which serves Mont Blancs, my favorite dessert. I was first taken there by a very glamorous couple when it was called Rumplemayer's, a sister restaurant to a patisserie of the same name on 59th Street in New York, down the street from the Plaza. The glamorous couple and I had been staying at the same home on the Riviera.

It was just after my first, brief, marriage, and I had taken what money I had to go to England and France. I stayed at the YWCA in London, ate a few meals with friends of friends, and walked around Mayfair and Kensington, not knowing I would return there to live in a few years' time. Then I flew to Nice, the Riviera being my introduction to France. My first meal was lunch with the glamorous people—he was a TV star for CBS and she was equally awe-inspiring. We ate at a famous restaurant, La Colombe d'or, which I'd first heard of in a movie, looking down into a valley of trees and tiled roofs, surrounded by original art on the walls.

My beau, Chester, was what I call a "grandfather clause"—a previous relationship that had special rules. He too had married and divorced and moved to France since last we had seen each other. But we rendezvoused there, and after an idyllic week of sun and sand, where I met tiny olives mixed with tiny tomatoes as a beach snack, my first omelette, and buttery non-iceberg lettuce, I rode with the glamorous couple to Paris. There, we went to Rumplemayer's, where I had their famous hot chocolate and pastries and was entranced by their painted walls and decor. The next time I was in Paris it had been purchased and was called Angelina's. Their Mont Blanc became my favorite dessert and remains so still.

It took an online recipe attributed to Angelina's for chestnut purée, coupled with my meringue recipe, for my assistant Jinny Ridall, to unlock the secrets. May it become your favorite dessert too. Oh, I never saw the famous couple again, Chester popped into my life with varying endearments, between then, one marriage, and partway to the last and final one before I had the sense to see what a cad he was. It just goes to show that a good recipe for a meringue can outlast a man's affections.

# ANGELINA'S MONT BLANC

Angelina's is a most glorious restaurant on the Rue de Rivoli in Paris. At one time it was called Rumplemayer's, and there was one in New York across from Central Park as well. Angelina was the name of the owner's daughter, and the name was changed sometime in the 1970s.

MAKES 8

1 recipe Swiss or Traditional Meringue
(page 175 or page 173)

**CHESTNUT PURÉE**

MAKES ABOUT 3 CUPS, OR SUBSTITUTE 2 TO 3 CUPS
STORE-BOUGHT CHESTNUT PURÉE

1 ¼ pounds roasted shelled chestnuts

1 vanilla bean, split

⅓ cup granulated sugar

**MASCARPONE CREAM**

1 cup heavy cream

4 ounces mascarpone

2 tablespoons confectioners' sugar, plus more
for dusting

1 teaspoon vanilla

Prepare Swiss Meringue recipe as directed (page 175). When you are ready to bake, preheat oven to 200 degrees. Prepare a baking sheet by lining with parchment paper. Draw eight 3 ½-inch circles on the parchment paper as your guide for piping the meringues. Place in pastry bag fitted with ½-inch plain tip and pipe eight small rounds onto prepared sheet (see piping directions in the Traditional Simple Meringues recipe, page 173). Bake 2 hours, or until meringue is firm to the touch. If meringues brown during baking, reduce heat. Transfer meringues to rack and let cool.

Meanwhile, make the chestnut puree. Add chestnuts to a medium pot and cover with water. Scrape the seeds from the vanilla bean; add bean and seeds to the pot. Bring to the boil over high heat. Reduce heat to low, cover, and simmer until chestnuts are very tender, about 30 minutes. Rinse the vanilla bean pod and reserve for another purpose. Drain chestnuts, then add to the bowl of a food processor and purée until almost smooth.

In a small saucepan, bring ⅓ cup sugar and ¾ cup water to the boil to make a thin sugar syrup. Set aside to cool. When cool, stream syrup into the chestnut purée while the motor is running. It should be thin enough to pipe through a pastry bag but still thick enough to hold its shape (you may not need all

> CONTINUED

the syrup). If using canned puree, sweeten to taste with sugar syrup, making sure it is thin enough to be piped. Fit pastry bag with a 1/10-inch plain tip and fill with purée, or use a squeeze bottle.

Beat cream in a mixing bowl until medium peaks form, and then add mascarpone, sugar, and vanilla. Beat until stiff peaks form. Cut a small slit in one corner of a plastic bag, or use a plastic or pastry bag with a tip. Position the bag in a sturdy mug or glass, and fold the top third of the bag down around the outside of the container. Scoop the cream from the bowl into the bag until it is half full. Pull up the surrounding part of the bag and twist the cream-free top to keep the cream from gushing out. Hold the twisted part of the bag with the dominant hand, and position the fingers of the other hand at the bottom tip. Push from the top.

Arrange cooked meringues on parchment paper. Squeeze and spread a thin layer of chestnut puree on top, pipe mascarpone cream in a tall mound on top of each, then pipe chestnut puree in a bird's-nest shape all around the edges and the top of the cream. Sprinkle with confectioners' sugar and chill until serving time.

# CLASSIC CARAMEL CAKE

A popular national recipe in the 20th century, it is mostly prepared by Southern bakers and cooks and claimed as our own. The Caramel (burnt sugar) Icing was traditionally made in an iron skillet. Only a small amount of sugar is caramelized for the icing, but it flavors the whole mixture, giving the icing a grainy texture from the undissolved sugar. Some people prefer it that way. Heavy cream (my favorite) is preferred over half-and-half for its higher fat content, which prevents curdling. Use a candy thermometer to accurately judge the soft-ball stage. Keep warm by putting the bowl of icing in a pan of hot water until finished icing the cake, or it can be microwaved to reheat, checking in 10- to 20-second increments to make sure it does not overcook. For best results, the icing should be spreadable, like peanut butter. A thermometer, whether instant-read or candy, makes any sugar work easier. Sugar work is much more difficult on a rainy day because of the relationship between sugar and humidity.

MAKES 1 (9-INCH) ROUND 3-LAYER CAKE OR 1 (9 X 13 X 2-INCH) 2-LAYER CAKE

1 ½ cups unsalted butter, room temperature

2 cups granulated sugar

5 large eggs

3 cups all-purpose or cake flour

¼ teaspoon salt

½ teaspoon baking powder

1 ¼ cups milk

1 teaspoon vanilla extract

1 recipe Caramel Icing (page 184)

Position rack in the center of the oven and preheat to 325 degrees. Butter and flour three 9-inch cake pans or two 9 x 13-inch pans. Line the bottoms with parchment or waxed paper. Butter and flour the paper.

Cut the butter into 1-inch pieces, add to the bowl of a stand mixer fitted with a rotary whisk, and beat on low speed until soft. Increase the speed and whisk for 1 or 2 minutes, until it looks like lightly whipped cream. Add the sugar 1 tablespoon at a time, starting on low and increasing speed until well whipped, about 7 or 8 minutes. Beat in the eggs one at a time, beating after each addition.

Sift together the dry ingredients onto a large piece of waxed paper. Add a third of the flour mixture to the egg mixture and beat to incorporate, then half the milk and beat; repeat, ending with flour. Add

> CONTINUED

the vanilla extract and beat until smooth. Pour the batter evenly into the cake pans. Tap the pans once against the counter to remove any air bubbles and smooth the top of the batter.

Bake 35 to 45 minutes, until a toothpick inserted in the middle comes out clean. The internal temperature of the cake should be 190 to 195 degrees on an instant-read thermometer.

Move the pans to a wire rack to cool completely. Carefully run a knife around the inside of the pans to loosen the cakes. Turn the pans upside down over pieces of parchment paper. Remove pans and peel off the paper. The cakes may be made ahead to this point. Well-wrapped, they can be frozen up to 2 months.

Spread with Caramel Icing (below), following icing directions on page 187.

# CARAMEL ICING

Combining a small amount of caramel sauce with a sugar syrup produces this caramel icing.

MAKES 3½ TO 4 CUPS

3 ¼ cups granulated sugar, divided

1 tablespoon light corn syrup

¼ cup water

½ cup unsalted butter, softened

¼ teaspoon baking soda

1 teaspoon vanilla extract

1 ½ cups cream, half-and-half, or milk, divided

Heat ¼ cup of the sugar with the corn syrup and water in a small saucepan over medium heat until dissolved. Proceed to cook until it turns a deep copper-amber color, watching carefully and swirling the pot over the heat as necessary to distribute the color evenly. A small portion may appear burnt— don't worry unless the whole mixture seems burnt and has a burnt odor. If the whole mixture tastes burnt, discard and start over. This is the caramel.

Meanwhile, on low heat, dissolve the remaining 3 cups sugar with the butter, baking soda, vanilla, and 1 cup cream or milk in a large, heavy pan or Dutch oven. When dissolved, bring to a simmer just until little bubbles appear around the outside of the pan. Take care not to let it boil over.

> CONTINUED

Cover both hands with oven mitts or cloths to protect them from caramel splashes. Add a small portion of the cream or milk mixture to the caramel and bring to the boil to dissolve; pour it into the simmering milk mixture. If necessary to remove all the caramel from the pan, repeat this step. Bring the mixture to the boil and boil rapidly to the soft-ball stage (240 degrees on a candy thermometer), stirring constantly.

Carefully remove pan from the heat and place in a large roasting pan filled with enough cold water to stop the caramel cream from cooking. Transfer caramel cream quickly to the bowl of a stand mixer fitted with a rotary whisk, and beat until very thick and creamy. It should look and spread like peanut butter. If necessary, add a bit more of the cream to make it spreadable. If it is too cold to spread, place the bowl in a pan of hot water to warm up, and add a bit more cream if necessary. It also may be briefly warmed in the microwave as well, if transferred out of the metal bowl. Spread the icing on the cake. See page 187 for how to ice a cake.

**VARIATIONS: ORANGE CARAMEL CAKE:** Substitute 8 ounces sour cream for the milk and use orange extract instead of vanilla. Add ½ cup orange juice and 2 teaspoons grated orange rind, no white attached, to the icing ingredients when bringing them to a simmer.

- Decorate the top and sides with pecan halves.

**T I P :** To clean the caramel pan, add hot water, bring to the boil, and slosh around to dissolve the caramel. If necessary, continue to boil until caramel is dissolved. Caramel should be well diluted before pouring water into the sink so it doesn't harden in the drains.

# HOW TO ICE A CAKE

I think it is charming for home cakes to have a dome, declaring they are "homemade." When necessary, even out domes or overbrowned layers with a sharp serrated knife. If they aren't burned, keep the trimmings and make them into crumbs for decorating or into cutouts to keep children (and the cook) happy until it is time to eat the cake.

The tops of cakes will frequently crumb. Cake bakers usually remove this crumb with a pastry brush before icing. Move the prettiest layer to a rack set over waxed paper to catch icing drippings. Ice the cake layer by ladling or spooning a portion of the icing into the middle of the cake. Use a long spatula to spread, starting in the middle and working out to the sides. Wait to ice the sides until the cake is assembled. Keep the drippings in case more icing is needed for the bottom and middle layers. (It can't be used for the sides, as it will have cake crumbs in it.)

Divide the remaining icing onto the number of layers left to ice, remembering to save some for the sides. Choose the least desirable layer as the bottom layer. Any broken layer should be in the middle. After the bottom layer is determined, move it to a cardboard cake round. If using a cake plate, make spokes with 5 x 3-inch strips of parchment or waxed paper on the serving plate, extending slightly, to catch the icing from dripping onto the plate. Ice as above, remembering that too much icing on the bottom two layers will cause the cake to slide.

Ice middle layer on a cake rack, then move on top of bottom layer. Top with the pretty layer, which is already iced. Spread icing over the sides if there is sufficient remaining. Slide out the strips of paper and tidy up the plate.

If icing is too stiff to spread smoothly, recheck the recipe to determine if ingredients were measured carefully, and adjust as needed. If it is simply too cold to spread, warm it quickly and carefully over low heat or in the microwave. If the icing is runny, chill slightly first, then try to add some of the thickest ingredient to make it firmer.

# ORANGES IN CARAMEL

Originally a recipe from Chef Henri Pellaprat, co-founder of Le Cordon Bleu Paris, this made its way into the repertoire of Dione Lucas, Rosemary Hume, Julia Child, and others of his students, and then on to their students, of which I am one, and then to all of our students. It is always a winning dessert. Accompany with a small cookie if desired, or serve with a ginger snap and whipped cream.

SERVES 6

1 recipe Caramel Sauce (page 190)

6 oranges, plus rind

Prepare Caramel Sauce as directed (this may be done a day ahead).

Grate the rind of the oranges, leaving no white attached to the rind, or peel strips with a potato peeler and slice into thin julienne strips. Remove remaining rind and pith, and slice the oranges horizontally into rounds; remove the seeds.

Pour Caramel Sauce as needed over the oranges up to a day before serving. Sprinkle on the grated or julienned orange peel. Cover with plastic wrap. Serve individually or in a large bowl.

**VARIATIONS:** Add candied ginger and/or candied orange peel (page 191) as well as, or in place of, the grated rind. Or add candied ginger to the caramel sauce.

> CONTINUED

# CARAMEL SAUCE

MAKES 1 TO 2 CUPS

1 cup granulated sugar or a mixture of brown and granulated sugar, or all brown sugar, or honey

¼ cup light corn syrup

2 cups water, divided

Heat the sugar in a saucepan with the corn syrup and 1 cup water over low heat, without boiling, stirring once or twice if necessary to completely dissolve the sugar. (There may be a little "sugar scum" on top, but the sugar on the bottom should be dissolved.) If there are sugar crystals on the side, brush down the sides of the pan, without touching the syrup, using a brush dipped in water. Place a pan of cold water next to the stove large enough to hold the saucepan if needed.

Once the sugar is completely dissolved, bring to the boil over high heat. This is the sugar syrup. Boil steadily until large bubbles form on the surface. Watch closely as the caramel turns from bursting bubbles to little bubbles then caramel. Cover hands or use an oven mitt, and tip the pan once it begins to color so the sugar colors uniformly. When it turns amber, remove from the heat. It will continue to bubble. If it becomes as dark as mahogany, carefully move it to a pan of water to cool it down immediately and stop the cooking. (Be careful of the bubbling water and sugar.) This is now a "caramel." Left alone to cool, it will harden.

To continue making the sauce, wipe the bottom of the pot dry if necessary and return to the heat, adding the remaining cup of water. Return to the boil. If part of the caramel syrup has solidified, stir with a clean wooden spoon so the caramel will be evenly distributed. Bring back to the boil, and boil until reduced by one-fourth and slightly syrupy. Cool, pour into another container, and chill. This will last several weeks covered in the refrigerator.

# CANDIED CITRUS RIND

For citrus aficionados, this is a temptation. Store judiciously. Use various citruses, or just one type, as below. Serve whole, or chop and use in cakes, fruit cakes, and any time you would use candied ginger.

MAKES 2 CUPS (10 SLICES PER ORANGE)

3 large oranges with thick skin

4 cups water, plus more for boiling rind

1 ½ cups granulated sugar, divided

2 tablespoons light corn syrup

Using a knife or vegetable peeler, peel rind from the orange, not getting any of the white. Add the peels to a 3-quart pot of cold water, making sure the water completely covers the rind. Bring the water to the boil, and boil for about 30 seconds. Drain in a colander and rinse the rind under cold water. Return rind to the clean pot and cover with cold water. Repeat the boiling and rinsing process.

After rinsing the rind the second time in cold water, add rind to a clean pot along with 4 cups water, ¾ cup of the sugar, and the corn syrup. Cook over low heat until the sugar is dissolved. Bring to a gentle boil and cook for 1 to 1 ½ hours. When done, the rind should be transparent, and there should be just enough syrup to coat all the pieces.

Spread remaining sugar on a cookie sheet and roll the rind in the sugar. Allow to dry on a wire rack for 1 hour or more. Turn pieces over with tongs and make sure they are dry before storing. Allow to sit if not completely dry. Store in the refrigerator.

# NATHALIE'S CREAM PUFFS

Nearly every European nation has a version of this dough, which in French is called pâte á choux. It can be baked, fried, boiled, or mixed with other foods to make another product altogether. A version was in Martha Washington's cookbook as well as Thomas Jefferson's. I invented this version thirty years ago after seeing a pastry made with a similar technique in an antiquarian cookbook and have used it ever since. It makes a roux first, then the liquid is added, it is stirred until thoroughly cooked, and then the eggs are beaten in to incorporate air. It's a handy dough to master, as usually the ingredients are readily available and inexpensive. The recipe doubles easily, and the cooked puffs freeze well in a sturdy airtight container.

MAKES 20 PUFFS, DEPENDING ON SIZE

1 recipe Pâte á Choux

1 recipe Diplomat Cream (page 195)

1 recipe Chocolate Sauce, optional (page 197)

### PÂTE Á CHOUX

6 tablespoons unsalted butter

1 cup minus 2 tablespoons bread flour

1 teaspoon salt

1 tablespoon granulated sugar, optional

1 cup water

3 large eggs

2 egg whites

1 egg yolk mixed with 1 teaspoon water, for glaze

Melt the butter in a heavy 10- to 12-inch frying pan over medium heat. Whisk together flour, salt, and optional sugar. Stir into the melted butter over medium heat until the butter and flour come together. Continue stirring until the butter-flour mixture is smooth. Add the water and continue stirring until the mixture comes together. At first it will be paste-colored. When it pulls together into a thick glob and resembles well-buttered thickish mashed potatoes, with no streaks of white, indicating the flour has been sufficiently cooked, remove from the heat. In a frying pan this should take about 5 minutes.

Cool slightly. Fit a food processor with the metal blade. Add the paste. Mix the eggs and egg whites together in a small bowl. Add the eggs ¼ cup at a time to the paste, pulsing after each addition. (Or beat with an electric hand mixer or a sturdy spoon.) Pulse or beat until the dough is glossy and drops slowly from a spoon. There may be some liquid remaining. Just discard any extra liquid. At this point, add cheese or any other flavorings as desired (see variations, page 194). The mixture may be made ahead to this point and refrigerated tightly covered for several days. Bring back to room temperature before baking.

> CONTINUED

Preheat oven to 350 degrees.

Line a rimmed baking sheet with parchment or waxed paper. Use a small amount of the dough to hold down the four corners of the paper. Snip a small corner off one end of a plastic or pastry bag and fit with a tip. (Using a pastry tube makes a more polished end product but is not crucial.) Position the bag in a sturdy mug or glass, and fold the top third of the bag down around the outside of the container. Scoop the dough from the bowl into the bag until half full. Pull up the surrounding part of the bag and twist the dough-free top to keep the dough from gushing out. Hold the twisted part of the bag with the dominant hand, and position the fingers of the other hand at the bottom tip. Push from the top.

Pressing from the tops and sides of the bag, pipe the pastry into nearly identical rounds or other shapes onto the parchment paper. The pastries may vary in size and shape from baking sheet to baking sheet, but those on each sheet should be consistent. Brush puffs with egg glaze and lightly press the tops with a fork to flatten. Bake one pan at a time until medium brown with no paste-colored streaks showing, about 30 minutes. Remove from oven, insert a needle, skewer, or small knife tip and pierce a hole in the side or bottom of each pastry. Return to oven. Reduce heat to 325 and bake 10 minutes more. Test by removing one puff and setting aside to cool.* Return the batch to the oven as needed, continuing to test. Adjust baking time for remaining pastry. Remove and cool briefly on a rimmed baking sheet before moving to a rack. The puffs may be kept covered a day or so at room temperature, or frozen for up to 3 months. Recrisp in a 350-degree oven for about 4 to 5 minutes before filling if they have become soggy. Fill as desired with Diplomat Cream before serving. Serve with optional Chocolate Sauce if desired.

To fill, insert a pastry tip into the previously cut hole and pipe in a smooth mixture, or split the puff in half horizontally, remove any undercooked centers, and fill with desired mixture. Replace the top and serve with chocolate sauce, if desired.

*Most novices tend to underbake the dough. Before the pan is returned to the oven, set one puff aside. As it cools, it will become softer. If it is not thoroughly cooked, it will become very soft and collapse to the touch. This indicates it was not cooked thoroughly. Return to pan in the oven. After 10 minutes, remove another puff and repeat the test.

### VARIATIONS: SWEET AND SAVORY CREAM PUFF VARIETIES

- For sweet cream puffs, add 1 tablespoon granulated sugar to the dough before baking. Bake quarter-sized, split, and fill with Diplomat Cream (page 195), whipped heavy cream, custard, or lemon curd. Sprinkle with confectioners' sugar or dip in caramel.

- For savory cream puffs, add ¾ cup grated Gruyère cheese to the dough. Pipe dime-sized puffs and bake for a shorter time, to serve alone or to add to soups. Bake quarter-sized, split, and fill with chicken salad or other savory fillings.

- Both sweet and savory cream puffs accommodate a variety of fillings, from custard and sauces to tasty chopped items such as berries, nuts, or olives. These ingredients can also be added to the batter, as can cocoa or curry powder, when making small puffs as tasty little bites

# DIPLOMAT CREAM

I can't remember making a Diplomat Cream until Gabrielle Hamilton introduced one in the *New York Times Magazine*. I've taken it as my own, as it prevents weeping and keeps cream puffs and other pastries from getting as soggy as they do with whipped cream or pastry cream.

MAKES ABOUT 2 CUPS, ENOUGH FOR ABOUT 12 GOLF-BALL SIZED CREAM PUFFS. TO FILL CROQUEMBOUCHE (PAGE 198), THREE BATCHES WILL BE NEEDED.

1 cup milk

1 vanilla bean, split, seeds scraped, both reserved

¼ cup granulated sugar, divided

3 egg yolks

1 ½ tablespoons cornstarch

Pinch of salt

1 tablespoon cold butter

¼ cup plus 1 tablespoon heavy cream, divided

½ teaspoon granulated gelatin

1 tablespoon tap water

Combine milk, vanilla bean and seeds, and 2 tablespoons of the sugar in a small saucepot. Heat almost to the boil (small simmering bubbles will appear around the edge of the pan) over medium heat. Remove from heat.

In a heatproof mixing bowl, whisk together remaining 2 tablespoons sugar, egg yolks, cornstarch and salt until thick and creamy and pale yellow. Whisk the hot milk into the yolk mixture, then pour through a strainer, if necessary, to catch any cooked bits of egg, then back into the saucepot. Return pot to the stove and whisk constantly over medium-high heat until it bubbles and thickens, about 90 seconds. Remove from heat and pour contents back into the bowl, again through a strainer. Move the bowl over

> CONTINUED

a panful of ice to cool slightly. Whisk in the cold butter while the mixture is still warm. When the pastry cream has cooled completely, add 1 or 2 tablespoons heavy cream to it to make it loose and soft when incorporating the gelatin. Set aside off the ice.

In a small microwave-safe bowl, sprinkle gelatin over the tap water evenly to soften. Break up any clumps, then microwave for 10 or 15 seconds to dissolve completely. If no microwave is available, add the water to a metal measuring cup or small pan, sprinkle in the gelatin and let sit a few minutes until it thickens evenly. Melt and dissolve over a very low heat until completely liquid. Taking care the bowl is not colder than the ingredients, as the gelatin will head for the coldest spot when dissolved, stir dissolved gelatin mixture into the cool pastry cream, making sure there are no clumps of undissolved gelatin. If there are, either remove completely and discard, or remove and redissolve in microwave or pan as before and re-add, stirring as before. Return to top of the pan of ice and stir with a spatula until the liquid is cool. Remove from the ice once cool.

Whip remaining ¼ cup cold heavy cream to peaks the texture of the pastry cream and fold into the chilled pastry cream, blending thoroughly. Cover with plastic wrap and chill in a refrigerator until ready to use.

**VARIATION:** Flavor with orange liqueur, Madeira, sherry, or other liquid.

## STRAINING A CUSTARD

Not all egg dishes need straining, but "boiled" custards have two reasons for doing so: 1) removing the chalazae, the "stringy" part of the egg whites, and 2) the possibility of some overcooked eggs lurking on the bottom and sides of the pan. Straining cools down the custard as well as removing the less desirable bits and the bean pod. Unfortunately it may also remove the vanilla seeds, which lend a bit of character to the sauce.

# CHOCOLATE SAUCE

This is a foolproof chocolate sauce. Of course, if a better chocolate is available or bitter chocolate is preferred, it can be substituted.

½ cup heavy cream

3 heaping tablespoons semisweet
  chocolate chips

Heat the cream in a heavy pan on the stove, or in the microwave until hot but not boiling. When hot, add the chocolate and continue to cook over low heat until the chocolate is melted and smooth. Spoon hot sauce over cream puffs or set aside until needed. It will keep in the refrigerator covered for several weeks. Reheat over low heat or in the microwave if necessary.

# CROQUEMBOUCHE

My oldest nearly daughter Audrey married a Frenchman in France, where this was served at the dinner following her wedding. There are conical molds available, but free-form towers have a less formal, more welcoming look. Some croquembouche are made with a base or a pie or puff pastry round, which enables one to carefully move the croquembouche as necessary. Spun sugar adds a spectacular finish. The presentation plate should be one that can be immersed in hot water to dissolve any caramel adhering to it. I used to use one of silverplate, as it was sturdy and easy to dissolve the caramel.

MAKES ONE 10-INCH PYRAMID TO FEED ABOUT 15-20 PEOPLE

60 quarter-sized Nathalie's Cream Puffs (page 193) filled with Diplomat Cream (page 195)

3 cups granulated sugar

3 tablespoons light corn syrup

1 cup water

Caramel Cage (page 200), optional

Set cream puffs on parchment paper strips on a serving plate (see "How to Ice a Cake," page 187).

Make the caramel "glue": Add the sugar and corn syrup to the water and heat until dissolved over medium heat in a heavy saucepan without boiling. Bring to the boil and boil until it turns a rich amber color, about 20 to 30 minutes. Remove from heat and allow to cool just slightly. (See Caramel Sauce page 190 for more directions.)

Working quickly while the caramel is still warm and liquefied, using metal tongs, a long fork, or a gloved hand, dip the bottom side of one cream puff into the caramel, then dip the top. Place on the serving dish, bottom down. Continue dipping and moving to form a 10-inch circle of dipped cream puffs on the plate as a base. Another circle of caramelized puffs can be added inside this circle to create an extra-sturdy base for the pyramid. Continue to build by dipping another cream puff bottom. This layer will be smaller than the base layer, with each puff added in the center of two puffs below. Working quickly, add another puff adjacent and glued to the first, and also in between two base puffs. If the puffs are not adhering, it may be that the puffs need to be re-dipped, with the sides as well as the bottoms coated. Continue until the smaller round is on top of the base. If the caramel hardens, reheat over low to medium heat until liquid. Keep making rounds from the puffs and caramel, gluing each round into place on top of the one below, each round smaller than the previous one. When finished in a pyramid, brush the visible portions of the puffs with the extra caramel until shiny, securing any loose puffs with caramel, and remove parchment strips.

# SPUN CARAMEL CAGE

To finish the croquembouche, make a spun sugar cage. Move two wooden spoons to the edge of a countertop or table and tape the bowls of the spoons, facing down, onto the counter, with the wooden handles protruding out. Oil the handles to prevent the caramel from sticking to them. Spread newspaper underneath the work area to catch the caramel as it drips. (Or take a cue from photographer Hélène Dujardin. She does this on the counter above an open dishwasher door, which catches the drips. Then close and run through a cycle for easy cleanup!)

1 cup granulated sugar

1 tablespoon light corn syrup

⅓ cup water

Dissolve the sugar and corn syrup by heating with the ⅓ cup water. Once thoroughly dissolved, bring to the boil and continue to boil until the syrup has reached the hard-crack stage (between 295 and 310 degrees). Remove from heat and allow to cool slightly. Dip a fork or metal whisk into the warm caramel and make generous circles under and over the two spoon handles, creating a large nest of the golden strings. Don't worry if any break as they harden. Just start another string and continue making the large circles. Use two hands to carefully move the bird's nest to surround the croquembouche. Start at the top and work down, as the caramel circle may not be large enough to surround the croquembouche if the initial circles were not large enough. It will be pretty whatever is done!

Carefully store the croquembouche until ready to serve, preferably in a refrigerator or cold place. To serve, use two spoons to remove the puffs individually to small plates, 2 or 3 puffs per serving. Serve with some of the spun sugar.

# ACKNOWLEDGMENTS

With sincere thanks to all who helped, directly or indirectly, over the years in the creation of this book:

Jack Bass and Kitty, who had to put up with not interrupting me

Kate Almand

Angelina's restaurant

Rose Beranbaum

Pat Conroy

Ma-Ma Dupree

Alma Friedman

Lauren Furey

Gabrielle Hamilton

Marcella Hazan

Rhoda Kreiser

Nicole Marriner

Deni Seibert

David Tanis

Anne Willan

Virginia Willis

Marion Wright

Ray Wright

Food photographer Hélène Dujardin, and food stylists Angie Moser and Anna Hampton; special thanks to recipe tester Jenni Ridall

Previous publications and editors:

*Atlanta Journal-Constitution*

*Atlanta Magazine*

*Post and Courier* Food section

*Brown's Guide to Georgia*

*Los Angeles Times Syndicate*

Fred Brown

Dudley Clendenin

Russ Parsons

And especially Cynthia Graubart and Madge Baird

# INDEX

# METRIC CONVERSION CHART

| VOLUME MEASUREMENTS | | WEIGHT MEASUREMENTS | | TEMPERATURE CONVERSION | |
|---|---|---|---|---|---|
| U.S. | Metric | U.S. | Metric | Fahrenheit | Celsius |
| 1 teaspoon | 5 ml | 1/2 ounce | 15 g | 250 | 120 |
| 1 tablespoon | 15 ml | 1 ounce | 30 g | 300 | 150 |
| 1/4 cup | 60 ml | 3 ounces | 90 g | 325 | 160 |
| 1/3 cup | 75 ml | 4 ounces | 115 g | 350 | 180 |
| 1/2 cup | 125 ml | 8 ounces | 225 g | 375 | 190 |
| 2/3 cup | 150 ml | 12 ounces | 350 g | 400 | 200 |
| 3/4 cup | 175 ml | 1 pound | 450 g | 425 | 220 |
| 1 cup | 250 ml | 2 1/4 pounds | 1 kg | 450 | 230 |